PRIMARY
FOUNDATIONS

Physical education
AGES 7-9

Pauline Boorman
and Bob Bellew

CONTENTS

Authors
Pauline Boorman
and Bob Bellew

Editor
Simon Tomlin

Assistant editor
Roanne Davis

Series designer
Lynne Joesbury

Designer
Joy Monkhouse

Illustrations
Ray & Corinne
Burrows

Cover photograph
Martyn Chillmaid

Published by
Scholastic Ltd,
Villiers House,
Clarendon Avenue,
Leamington Spa,
Warwickshire
CV32 5PR
Text © Pauline Boorman
and Bob Bellew
© 2001
Scholastic Ltd

1 2 3 4 5 6 7 8 9 0
0 1 2 3 4 5 6 7 8 9

British Library Cataloguing-in-Publication Data
A catalogue record for this book is available from
the British Library.

ISBN 0-439-01842-0

Introduction

The importance of physical education

'Physical Education develops pupils' physical competence and confidence, and their ability to use these to perform in a range of activities. It promotes physical skilfulness, physical development and a knowledge of the body in action. It provides opportunities for pupils to be creative, competitive and to face challenges as individuals and in groups and teams. It promotes positive attitudes towards active and healthy lifestyles. Pupils learn how to plan, perform and evaluate actions, ideas and performances to improve their aptitudes, abilities and preferences, and make choices about how to get involved in lifelong physical activity.' (*The National Curriculum Handbook for Primary Teachers in England: Key Stages 1 and 2*, DfEE/QCA).

At a time when there are real concerns over the low levels of physical activity amongst British school children, when children are becoming heavier and fatter and are leading increasingly sedentary lifestyles, this statement highlights the important contribution of PE, not only to promoting healthy lifestyles but to the whole developmental process.

Movement is probably the most natural and spontaneous learning medium for children. It capitalises on their inherent playful enthusiasm for active involvement in everything around them. It is indeed the business of childhood and as such is an essential entitlement for all children and an integral part of a broad, balanced curriculum. Schools alone cannot meet the exercise needs of children, but they do have a responsibility to broaden and extend their physical experiences in a variety of contexts (indoors and outdoors, individually and with others, with a variety of equipment) and to help them to move safely, efficiently, imaginatively and with increasing control.

Movement involves three very different but complementary facets of learning: learning how to move, learning through movement and learning about movement.

Learning how to move

The development of physical literacy enables children to manage the everyday demands of living: to be co-ordinated and skilful, creative and expressive, sensitive and energetic in a variety of gross and fine motor activities. In every lesson, all children should have as much opportunity, experience and practice to develop their confidence and competence in these areas as possible.

It is the physical nature of this mode of learning that gives it its distinct identity and makes it unique in the school situation in the sense of being only specifically addressed in physical education. Yet its impact on all other areas of development on the whole learning process, as recent brain studies suggest, can be inestimable (sitting still is one of the more refined of physical skills).

Learning through movement
Links with other areas of the curriculum

We all learn by doing, and for young children particularly, practical experience is an essential ingredient for involvement, assimilation and understanding and often motivation. Through involvement in physical activities, children are presented with many opportunities to think, plan, remember, discuss, assess and solve problems, make decisions and use their judgement. These are skills that are relevant across the curriculum.

There are many ways of using movement as a way of extending, for example, mathematical, literacy, scientific or geographical understanding. It is essential, however, that this is not done in artificial or contrived ways, but in ways that genuinely contribute to understanding in other areas.

Links with personal and social education

Movement also has the potential for providing, extending and enhancing many activities that make demands on children's personal and social capabilities, for example in situations that call for interaction, sharing, taking turns, leading and following, collaboration, negotiation, responsibility and use of language. We know that physical activity affects feelings of well-being in a broader sense, but

activities that involve children in working in a group or team are not in themselves sufficient to ensure that children work effectively together. Children need to be helped in their interactions in ways that build on their sense of achievement and develop their self-esteem. It is important to develop their confidence and sense of achievement through varied and enjoyable practical activities.

Links with literacy and language

Throughout each unit of work, children are encouraged to listen and respond to others and to describe, explain and talk about their ideas and activities using appropriate language and some specialist vocabulary. It should be remembered, however, that physical education is primarily about doing, and opportunities for discussion should be brief and purposeful or take place primarily in the classroom, otherwise children might get bored, cold and restless.

Links with numeracy and science

The activities suggested in this book provide ideas for developing an understanding of shape, space and measures in a practical context, experiencing and coming to understand forces and motion in a meaningful way and developing an understanding of the effect of exercise on the body.

Learning about movement

With the current concerns about sedentary lifestyles, increasing obesity and the evidence of many hypokinetic diseases beginning in childhood, there are obvious implications for the primary teacher. The most important aspect of this focus on the body, and how it works, is the notion of a developing health awareness. The aspects particularly highlighted in the National Curriculum are each child's knowledge and understanding of fitness and health and of the effects of physical exercise on their bodies. By raising awareness of the role of physical activity in their lives and helping children towards feelings of satisfaction, exhilaration and fun derived from their sense of progress and achievement in physical education, it is hoped that these activities will encourage participation in the full sense of the word (thinking and doing) and that children can be helped to develop positive attitudes and a commitment to physical activity; to make reasoned, informed and healthy lifestyle choices.

About *Primary Foundations PE*

Through activities in dance, gymnastics, games, athletics, outdoor and adventurous activities and swimming, this book attempts to address the requirements of the curriculum and involve children in movement in a meaningful and practical way, in enjoyable and purposeful physical activity.

The units suggest ideas and detail ways in which practical activities can be developed and enhanced within a unit of work or series of lessons.

For each of the core areas of PE (games, dance and gymnastics), two aspects are developed in greater depth. The chapters suggest alternative activities or develop those outlined in the QCA schemes. One unit for swimming, for those schools that choose to teach it during this phase of Key Stage 2, and one unit each of athletics and outdoor and adventurous activities are also included. Each unit of work can be used to plan half a term's work for the area it covers: 30–45 minutes of activity per lesson. The units:

● provide a basis for developing and extending physical literacy… enhancing each child's movement repertoire and vocabulary in the core areas

● use a combination of exploratory, suggested, guided and directed activities to enable children to practise and develop their skills

● provide links with other areas of the curriculum.

It is important that the ideas given are seen as example plans. There is a great need for flexibility to suit the particular needs of each class or group. As with other areas of the curriculum, you will need to take account of children's previous experiences, current interests and developmental needs.

You will need to use a range of teaching styles and approaches; balancing activities that may be teacher-directed (as is often necessary at the beginning of a lesson to stimulate and involve the children) with activities in which children explore independently or collaborate with others and work together, gradually taking greater responsibility for their own learning.

The lessons suggested blend together some independent choices and directed activities with some challenges and activities to boost confidence. All have the potential for all sorts of learning through movement if one is open to the possibilities. It is hoped that you will be able to enjoy the activities with the children: observing, encouraging, teaching and monitoring their progress.

National Curriculum

'During Key Stage 2 pupils enjoy being active and using their creativity and imagination in physical activity. They learn new skills, use them in different ways and link them to make action phrases and sequences of movement. They enjoy communicating, collaborating and competing. They develop an understanding of how to succeed in different activities and learn how to evaluate and recognise their success.' (*The National Curriculum Handbook for Primary Teachers in England*, DfEE/QCA)

The activities in this book contribute towards the attainment target that sets out the development of the knowledge, skills and understanding that children of different abilities are expected to have attained by the end of Key Stage 2. The activities are designed to enhance the requirements of the National Curriculum, and provide examples of ways in which the QCA guidelines can be fleshed out.

Acquiring and developing skills
The units will help children to:
- explore ways of using their bodies in different contexts
- repeat skills, actions and ideas with increasing control, co-ordination and understanding
- practise and refine their actions
- manipulate and handle apparatus and equipment
- develop observation and social skills.

Selecting and applying skills, tactics and compositional ideas
Children will be encouraged to prepare and plan for physical activity by:
- choosing, selecting, adapting, varying and modifying actions and ideas
- remembering and linking together
- inventing and creating.

Evaluating and improving performance
Children will be prompted to:
- describe what they have done, what they liked and what they might do differently next time
- observe, analyse and appreciate the movement of others
- talk and think about what they have done and what they have achieved during the lessons.

Knowledge and understanding of fitness and health
Children will learn:
- how important it is to be active
- how to exercise safely, for example why we warm up before activity and cool down afterwards
- a greater awareness of how their bodies feel during different activities.

Encouraging independence and personal responsibility
The activities will help children to increase awareness of themselves and others and the context in which they are working, and develop an awareness of safety.

Inclusion

It is now statutory in physical education to provide effective learning opportunities for all children. Teachers are obliged to:

● consider the full requirements of the inclusion statement when planning for individuals or groups

● take account of children's religious and cultural beliefs and practices, such as allowing leggings for Muslim children but discouraging scarves which can be hazardous

● overcome any potential barriers to learning in physical education (some children may require adapted or alternative activities that have integrity and equivalence to the activities in the programmes of study and that enable children to progress, such as a way of travelling rather than jumping, or using a ball with a bell in it for a child who is partially sighted; specific support to enable them to participate in certain activities or types of movement, such as the buddy system, NSA support person; careful management of their physical regime to allow for specific medical conditions such as asthma and epilepsy)

● consider planning – where a support assistant is assigned to a child then they should be involved in the planning of activities

● in assessment, when children follow adapted or alternative activities, judge against level descriptions made in the context of the activities undertaken by the child.

For all children, there is a great need to recognise effort and progress rather than measure them against predetermined criteria.

Safety

Challenge and adventure are natural aspects of children's play. By their nature, many of the activities are hazardous and involve an element of risk. Such challenges within PE are both stimulating and demanding of each child's initiative, courage and determination, as well as their physical capabilities.

One of the most important priorities is to teach children to recognise and cope with the dangers around them in a constructive and positive way, whether it be raising their awareness of their use of skipping ropes, bats and throwing equipment in a limited space; of others as they move about; sharing the responsibility for using or handling apparatus; or preparing themselves for activity, for going outside, to the swimming pool or further afield. Simple rules can be discussed and established, with the children becoming fully involved in their implementation so they appreciate the need for them.

Trial and error is a necessary part of the learning process, but in the context of physical activity, it can often be a long and painful process. Safety precautions cannot remove all risks, but should eliminate all unnecessary dangers. Every opportunity should be used to help children develop a sense of safety, alerting them to ways in which their actions may impinge upon the safety of others.

The health and safety requirements of the current curriculum are quite general, so it is useful to look back on the more detailed requirements of the NCC Physical Education non-statutory guidance, June 1992, which states that within all activities, at whatever stage, 'pupils should be taught to:

● be concerned with their own and others' safety in all activities undertaken

● lift, carry and place equipment safely

● understand why particular clothing, footwear and protection are worn for different activities

● understand the safety risks of wearing inappropriate clothing, footwear and jewellery

● respond to instructions and signals in established routines, and follow relevant rules and codes.'
  To these must be added:

● Children should be helped to perform movement safely, for example resilient landings.

● All equipment should be checked and well maintained.

● Teachers need to be aware of any long standing or temporary medical conditions which may restrict or inhibit participation.

● Tasks and activities will need to be modified to suit the needs of a particular group or class.

● Everyone should be aware of the safety and first-aid procedures within school.

Whatever the situation or the activity, children should be able to learn how to move under all sorts of conditions with confidence and self-control, beginning to take care of themselves and becoming aware of their responsibilities towards others. When they are using equipment, help children to be aware of the space and other people.

Planning: phases of a lesson

In school, there are, of necessity, many constraints on the ways in which we can encourage children to be physically active. Often, class size, the space and resources available prevent an individualised approach, so the lessons in this book are set out to follow a common pattern.

Preparatory activities

These include all aspects of planning that involve the children.
● Classroom preparation, for example what to wear and changing routines; discussion of safety codes; organisation of groups; reminders about responsibility for apparatus and how this will be organised; discussion of intentions or related ideas.
● Physical preparation, for example activities that will warm up the body. These need to be purposeful and clearly related to the activities that are to follow.
● General preparation, for example response activities and use of space, listening and responding.

Development

Ideas and activities are then developed in a number of ways designed to engage children in many processes of learning and much physical activity. Through a variety of movement experiences, children can be helped to explore the wide range of possibilities and increase their movement vocabulary. Structured and focused tasks and activities will help to clarify ideas and actions and the main focus will be on helping children to think, understand and make judgements.

Climax

The process of practising, consolidating, selecting and/or combining actions will involve children in choosing, performing or sharing experiences. It may involve a sequence devised in dance, gymnastics on the floor or apparatus or a small-team game.

Conclusion

This will involve a calming or concluding activity in preparation for changing and returning to the classroom; a review, discussion or evaluation of activities, in the classroom after the activity.

Assessment

Although the sequence of progression through the stages of motor development is the same for most children, they do not progress at the same rate or an even rate, so there will be a wide range of differences in the ways children achieve various actions and movements. This is natural, as every child is unique. You will be aware that sometimes, in sheer excitement or in response to the demands of a situation, a child will use inconsistent or less advanced movements. Do not worry. Observe and enjoy the actions of each child and continue to create an atmosphere of success, fun and satisfaction.

Because of the fleeting nature of physical actions, detailed observation of a class of children constantly on the move is difficult. However, it is a good idea for you to get a general impression or overall feel for the class response. Ask yourself questions like:
● How do the children respond and listen to instructions and suggestions?
● How well do they think for themselves?
● How well do they follow others?
● How well do they combine thinking as an individual with working as part of a group?

- How well do they use the space? (Could they be encouraged to use it better?)
- Are they able to use different directions?
- Are they aware of other people when they use different directions?
- How well do they sustain energetic activity?

Continual review, with a focus on a few children at a time, is recommended. Try to watch how individual children respond and move. There will be times when you note achievement that is particularly significant and times when you look for specific responses. For example:

- Do they use the whole of the body when required? Which parts could they make more use of?
- How controlled are their movements? In which ways could they refine their movements?
- Can they observe, talk about and discuss their movements and ideas and those of others?

Dance

- How well do they respond to your voice, the rhythm, sounds or music?
- How imaginative and creative are they?
- Are they achieving the qualities required? When? If not, why not? What might help?
- How well do they use individual body parts? Do they use some parts more fully than others?
- Do they use different levels of their own volition?

Gymnastics

- How do they use and handle the apparatus? Imaginatively? Responsibly?
- How inventive are their actions?
- Can they clarify and hold their shapes in balance?
- Can they take their weight confidently on their hands?
- Can they select appropriate actions that answer the task set?
- Can they combine and link actions together in a sequence?

Games

- How confidently and agilely do they move about the space?
- How well are they developing their sending, receiving, striking and aiming skills?
- Are they beginning to use skills and tactics for attacking and defending?
- Can they make up and play a variety of simple team games?

At all times care should be taken to stress the positive aspects of the child's movement and to enjoy and encourage their attempts. There will be as many different responses as there are children and effort and progress should be acknowledged.

Differentiation

For most activities, differentiation will be *by outcome*. Tasks and problems are set which the children explore, investigate, try out, solve in different ways or are creative with, whatever their level of ability. Movement tasks and questions are open for individual interpretation, but limited enough for there to be a clear focus for attention.

Most tasks can also be *individualised*. Individual challenges can be suggested by you or made by the children. Additional support can be given, or modifications made, for individuals during the course of each lesson as you circulate and support, encourage, insist or challenge.

Sometimes there will be differentiation *by input* as you target particular children with special grouping, with suggestions (for example to make the task easier, to make it more difficult or challenging, to add an extra dimension) and with questions that vary in complexity or quality.

CHAPTER I

Gymnastics

In order to help children fully explore the potential of their bodies, it is necessary to suggest some challenges or place some limitations in movement. By providing a clear focus of attention, children can be involved in thinking about, performing and adapting their movements to the different suggestions. It is this response to movement problems which is so important. Children need time to play with ideas, to practise, consolidate and refine their favourite movements as well as to have new ones suggested to them. To explore the potential of different ideas and themes involves creativity, adaptation and review. Children are all individual and will come to each session with very different interests, past experiences, abilities and physiques. Progression, therefore, should be seen in a number of dimensions, not simply in the achievement of set gymnastic skills, but also with increasing awareness of the body, of others and of safety, developing observational skills and increasing quality. Challenge is part of the interest and excitement, and much is dependent upon the interest and manner of the teacher.

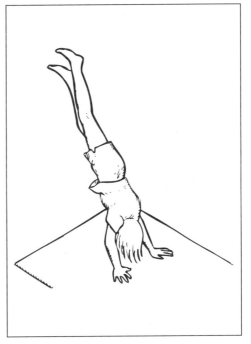

Lifting feet high

This unit gives particular emphasis to the position and shape of legs and feet in relation to the rest of the body. Through the actions of travelling, jumping and balancing, and by using different parts of the body (two feet, one foot, hands and feet, parts of the body such as the trunk), children will be encouraged to elevate their feet (sometimes one foot, sometimes both feet), thus exploring inversion.

Linking actions: bridging, sliding and jumping

With an emphasis on different ways of bridging (still, balanced shapes), this theme focuses on linking actions together. Using travelling actions such as sliding and jumping will help children to link together the still shapes and to incorporate changes of level in their sequences. They will be able to create and perform their own sequences with starting and finishing positions.

The units of work

Exploration and development of these ideas in each unit of work will help children to increase their movement vocabulary in gymnastics by encouraging and challenging them to find different solutions to the movement problems set or trying specific suggested actions.

By developing a theme gradually over a series of lessons, children can be helped to build up both confidence and competence, and be encouraged to respond imaginatively to the task. The limited focus will help the children to be clear about what they are trying to do and how they are doing it, as well as giving them scope for individual responses, whatever their ability.

Within each lesson, tasks have been selected for introduction or repetition as necessary, depending upon the children's responses. Attempts have been made to ensure that there is a balance between the introduction of new ideas and the choice and practise of familiar movements, and parts of the body used. Demonstrations can be chosen from children's responses to illustrate:
● range of ideas (to increase variety)
● use of space
● quality
● aspects of safety (such as resilient landings).

Encourage the children to try several different ways and then to select actions from those practised that will fulfil the task set. As part of the floor work and/or apparatus parts of the lesson, children can then be encouraged to refine their moves and to practise different ways of linking them.

Apparatus

It is essential that resources are easily accessible and that clear routines for getting out and putting away apparatus are adopted.

Children will enjoy taking responsibility for handling the apparatus, but they must be given clear guidance and direction. Whatever their previous experience, children will need to be taught or reminded to handle and use the apparatus carefully, emphasising the safety factors.

Make a plan of the apparatus to be used, checking what equipment is available. Make sure that it will support the theme.

Organisation of apparatus

Divide the class into six groups (to ensure all the children have a range of experiences and to help spacing). Each group should be responsible for handling the same apparatus throughout each unit.

Establish a fair and logical pattern of rotation of groups. For example, zigzag or clockwise (or straight swap if there are groups with similar apparatus). This will ensure that over a period of several lessons, the children can

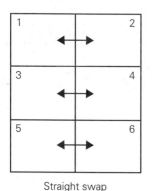

Straight swap

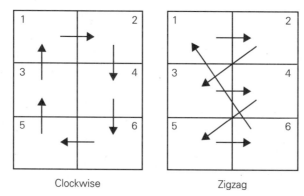

Clockwise   Zigzag

have a range of experiences, but a maximum of two apparatus changes in one lesson is recommended.

The zigzag is recommended so that the groups use different types of apparatus during a lesson. Alternatively, children could be encouraged to move freely to use different pieces or different combinations of apparatus.

Teach each group how to get out their apparatus correctly (appropriate positioning to carry it; bending their knees, not their backs; all looking in the direction they are moving in), and where to put it. (Use chalk marks initially to indicate the positioning of apparatus.)

Check the fixings and placement of apparatus before it is used, and encourage the children to do this too.

Using apparatus

There are two main methods for using apparatus:
● Free use. The children get out and put away the same apparatus but move freely around the whole area, working all the time and not standing waiting for turns. This gives children the opportunity to use their initiative and be independent in their choices.
● Groups. This is recommended (particularly when some apparatus is limited, for example ropes or climbing frame). Group organisation helps to ensure fair turns and will enable each group of children to have a similar amount of time on each arrangement. Each group will get out and put away their own apparatus but rotate to use other parts of the apparatus.

Whichever method you use:
● establish 'ground rules', for example, ensure that the children work quietly and considerately, using all the space, using the floor as well as the apparatus
● insist on a quiet working atmosphere, but discuss why with the children
● encourage and help the children to share space and equipment (using the floor space around the apparatus), particularly when there is limited apparatus
● establish a consistent routine for stopping, coming down and sitting away from the apparatus.

Encourage children to take responsibility for the safe handling, placement and checking of the apparatus, but always check it yourself too. To encourage maximum activity and independence and avoid queues, help children to use their apparatus thoughtfully in different ways, sharing the space available and moving carefully, responsibly and imaginatively.

Handling the Cave Southampton apparatus

Children in Years 3 and 4 should assist in getting out this apparatus. It is helpful to allocate this responsibility to one group for a unit of work or series of lessons (half a term) so that they become proficient and confident in handling it.

Before using the apparatus, check that the sockets for location bolts are clear and that any attachments (poles and ladders) are accessible and safely placed.

Safety is essential and explanation should focus on what should happen and why it is necessary:
● One child pulls down on each handle to release the frame (or trackway) and to lift it on to its wheels, keeping one hand on the handle and one hand on the frame (see Diagram 1). (NB. This must happen simultaneously with other linked panels.)
● Another child joins in to pull each panel out when you give the signal. It is important that they stand well back from the frame and watch their toes as the frame is pulled backwards (see Diagram 2).
● The bolt is lined up with the hole and the frame is then bolted to the floor as the handle is lifted (see Diagram 3).
● The straining wire is pulled, tightened and then secured by hooking it onto the lever and pressing it down to keep it in place (see Diagram 4).
● Apparatus fixings are checked by you and the children.
● Ladders or poles can then be fixed to the main frame. Two children can carry the poles (one at each end – see Diagram 5), but two further children are needed to hold the weight of the pole while the screws are tightened and

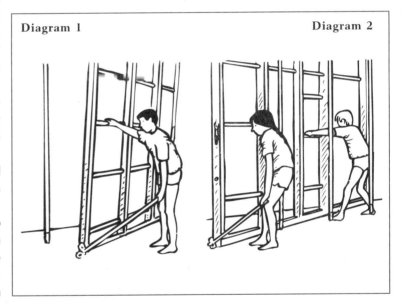

Diagram 1   Diagram 2

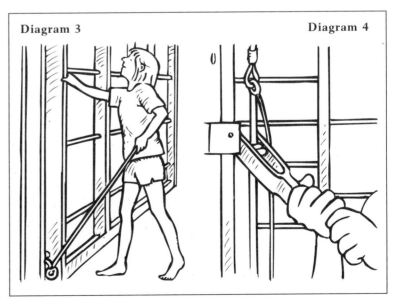

Diagram 3   Diagram 4

secured in the holes in the frame. Ladders can be carried on their sides (see Diagram 6) and placed flat on the floor before being lifted and fixed to the bar at the required height.

To put this apparatus away, the reverse procedure is adopted, checking that the bolt is resting in the wall bracket (top and bottom) to secure the frame against the wall for storage.

Three groups (of no more than five each) can use two panels of this apparatus (a bay each), provided that other apparatus (such as benches, mats, planks and ladders) are added, to help spacing. All the children will need reminders about spacing.

Diagram 5

Diagram 6

Lifting feet high

This unit explores different ways of travelling and balancing, with a particular emphasis on lifting one foot or both feet high. This will help children to explore the relationship between the feet and other parts of the body, and encourage elevation of the feet and thus inversion. It will help them to develop different travelling and balancing actions on different parts of their body (feet, hands and feet, other parts of body) and to refine the shape of the body in those actions.

The unit is divided into six sessions allowing approximately 30–45 minutes of activity per session. The first lesson will involve floor work and use of benches and mats. All other sessions will involve both floor work and apparatus work, but ideas can be modified to suit your school context.

The class can be divided into six groups to ensure good spacing and fair turns on each group of apparatus (approximately five children per group).

Please refer to the suggested apparatus plan on photocopiable page 124 for guidance on apparatus rotation before embarking on these sessions.

It is presumed that children will have had experiences of different ways of travelling and balancing on different parts of the body, and that they are developing their awareness of space, using the floor and apparatus.

UNIT: Lifting feet high

Enquiry questions	Learning objectives	Teaching activities	Learning outcomes
In what ways can we lift our feet high?	• Practise ways of travelling on feet, lifting them high. • Explore ways of balancing on both hands and one foot to make still shapes with one foot high. • Explore ways of balancing on large parts of the body, lifting one foot or both feet high. • Select and practise ways of balancing on the floor, mats and benches with feet high.	Warm-up: practising little jumps on the spot, gradually lifting feet higher; making a pattern of jumps. Floor work: walking, lifting feet high in different ways; trying other ways of travelling; practising ways of balancing on hands and feet, lifting one foot high. Apparatus work: trying balances with one foot or both feet high; travelling around, towards and along apparatus. Cool-down: jogging on the spot; lying down and relaxing.	Children: • listen and respond to the task set • understand the task • try to lift their feet high
Can we travel and balance with high feet?	• Refine ways of travelling on foot with one foot high. • Explore ways of travelling on the body, on the floor and apparatus, with one foot or both feet high. • Explore ways of balancing on the body and on hands and feet, on the floor and apparatus, with one foot or both feet high.	Warm-up: jogging on the spot then around the space, varying speed and direction; playing 'Statue stops'. Floor work: jumping on the spot, practising landings; practising travelling actions; practising balances on different parts of the body. Apparatus work: trying travelling actions on the mat, floor and bench; balancing on different parts of the body, lifting feet high. Cool-down: jogging slowly, lying down, stretching and relaxing.	• understand the task set • use different parts of their bodies • space well and use all parts of the apparatus
Can we think of more ways of lifting our feet high?	• Practise ways of travelling on feet with legs high. • Practise ways of resting on different parts of the body to lift feet high. • Practise ways of lifting feet high on apparatus. • Select some favourite actions to link together.	Warm-up: running on the spot and around the space; playing 'Statue stops'. Floor work: hopping with one foot held high in different ways; travelling on two hands and one foot; practising bunny jumps; balancing on different parts of the body; practising favourite actions. Apparatus work: trying different travelling actions towards, away from, along, on and off the apparatus; trying balances on the floor and apparatus. Cool-down: balancing on one leg; relaxing.	• take their weight safely on flat hands • space well on the apparatus • stretch their feet
How can we refine our high feet actions?	• Practise bunny jumps. • Try a sideways roll and/or a teddy bear roll, lifting and lowering the feet. • Select and try ways of lifting feet to make still shapes on the apparatus. • Observe and comment constructively on a partner's performance.	Warm-up: practising travelling actions; skipping, lifting feet high; playing 'Statue stops'. Floor work: practising bunny jumps; balancing on different parts of the body; rolling sideways; trying teddy bear roll; linking balances and travelling actions. Apparatus work: trying balances on the apparatus; practising travelling actions towards, away from, along, on and off apparatus; practise balances with part of the body on the apparatus. Cool-down: jumping gently; balancing on one foot; relaxing.	• think about lifting both feet or one foot high • use imaginative responses

Enquiry questions	Learning objectives	Teaching activities	Learning outcomes
Can we practise ways of lifting and lowering?	• Practise ways of lifting and then lowering feet and moving to another action. • Select and practise actions with one foot or both feet high, leading to a headstand. • Practise and refine ways of travelling and balancing on different parts of the apparatus with feet high. • Link actions to create a sequence on the floor and apparatus.	Warm-up: hopping on the spot and around the space; practising ways of travelling and jumping. Floor work: practising balances on hands and one foot; practising headstands; linking balances and travelling actions into a sequence. Apparatus work: practising ways of lifting feet and lowering them on different parts of the apparatus; practising bunny jumps and sideways travelling over parts of the apparatus; linking actions together. Cool-down: bunny jumping in different directions; tucking in, stretching out and relaxing.	• perform a bunny jump • select appropriate actions for their sequences
How can we link and refine our high feet actions?	• Practise ways of lifting feet high. • Explore ways of bunny jumping in different directions. • Practise and refine ways of lifting feet high to create a sequence on the floor and apparatus.	Warm-up: practising ways of moving around the space; trying scissor kicks. Floor work: practising striding and leaping; practising still balances; practising bunny jumps and cart-wheels; linking together favourite travelling actions. Apparatus work: practising favourite actions and linking to make a sequence on the apparatus; observing others perform a sequence. Cool-down: jogging slowly; trying bottom balance; relaxing.	• link their chosen actions into a sequence • describe their actions • say what they liked and what could be improved.

Cross-curricular links
Maths/science: by trying out and investigating with their own bodies and describing what they have done, children will develop a greater understanding of levels; they will also become increasingly aware of the functions of various body parts.

Resources
Apparatus for six groups; the apparatus plan on photocopiable page 124, modified as appropriate.

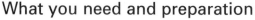

Lifting feet high

In what ways can we lift our feet high?
(30 mins)

What you need and preparation

You will need a mat and bench or box-top for each of six groups (of about five children).

In the classroom beforehand, discuss with the children the special requirements for getting to the hall and doing gymnastics (see Apparatus on page 10).

What to do

Warm-up
(4 mins)
Ensure the children are well spaced to start the warm-up. Ask them to try little bounces on the spot and encourage quiet, resilient, squashy landings, checking that there is good articulation of their ankles.

Start with toes hardly leaving the floor then encourage the children to lift their feet gradually a little higher off the ground.

Ask them to try the little bounces forwards and backwards and then in a another direction – side to side or diagonally (not travelling).

Encourage them to make a pattern of jumps as lightly as they can and to repeat them. This will raise the pulse and help them to remember a simple sequence of jumps (side to side, side to side, forward and back).

Floor work
(12 mins)
Ask the children to walk around the hall lightly on their feet. Encourage a bouncy step with arms in opposition to the feet, then encourage lifting feet further off the ground. Observe the children's responses and then select some demonstrations of different ways this could be done. For example, lifting their knees and therefore their feet high, lifting their feet with straight legs or lifting their feet up behind them.

Ask the children to choose one way of walking around the hall lifting their feet high. Ask them: *Can you get your feet even higher off the ground?*

Tell them to choose a different way of travelling on the feet – hopping, jumping, jogging – then encourage lifting feet further off the ground. Select some good examples for demonstration.

Ask everyone to use their hands and feet to make a still shape. Emphasise having strong, straight arms and flat hands to support the body.

Ask them to try another way, for example with tummy uppermost or back uppermost, then encourage them to lift one foot high. Encourage them to lift that foot up higher

Diagram 7

than the rest of the body. (See Diagram 7.) Can they try to use the other leg? Practise several different ways of making still shapes on two hands and one foot with one foot high. Can they lift the foot a bit higher?

Ask them to choose two shapes, making the foot the highest part. Can they link them together with a travelling action in between?

Lifting feet high

Now tell them to lie down and lift up one foot and then try both feet. Encourage a clear body shape and tension, and help the children to refine their shapes. (See Diagram 8.) Can they try this on another part of the body (sides, fronts, backs, shoulders)?

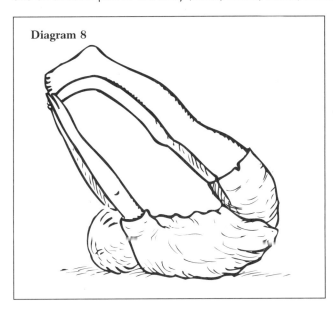

Diagram 8

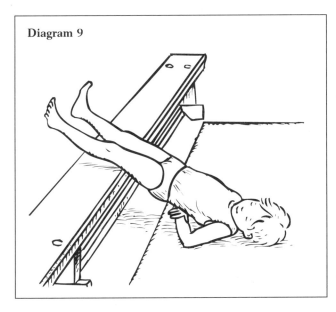

Diagram 9

Ask them to choose some of their favourite ways of travelling or balancing that they have tried and to practise them one after the other.

11 mins **Apparatus work**
Ask the children to get into six groups, and to get out one mat and one bench or box-top per group.

Advise them to find places on the mat or the floor, against or on the bench to try some still shapes with their feet high. Can they get one or both feet higher than the rest of their body? Can they sometimes use two hands and one foot, and sometimes other parts of their body, such as bottoms or shoulders? (See Diagram 9.) Encourage good use of space.

Now ask everyone to practise different ways of travelling around, towards or along their apparatus with one foot or both feet high. Encourage good spacing.

3 mins **Cool-down**
Ask the children to jog slowly on the spot, lifting their knees high, then gradually to lower their knees into a slow jog with the feet hardly leaving the ground. Ask them to lie down and relax and make their bodies go all floppy.

Classroom review
Encourage the children to describe some of the actions they tried today. Which actions did they try when their foot was the highest part of them?

Assessing learning outcomes
Are the children listening and responding to the task set? Do they understand the task? Are they trying to lift their feet high?

(30 mins) Can we travel and balance with high feet?

Learning objectives
● Refine ways of travelling on feet with one foot high.
● Explore ways of travelling on the body, on the floor and apparatus, with one foot or both feet high.
● Explore ways of balancing on the body and on hands and feet, on the floor and apparatus, with one foot or both feet high.

Lesson organisation
Brief discussion in the classroom; individual warm-up and floor work; apparatus practice in six groups; individual cool-down; teacher-led classroom review.

Vocabulary
balance
resilient
higher
lower

What you need and preparation

You will need apparatus for each of six groups; the apparatus plan on photocopiable page 124.

Discuss with children in the classroom the special requirements for getting out the apparatus (see Apparatus in the chapter introduction).

What to do

(3 mins) Warm-up

Ask the children to jog lightly on the spot, gradually varying the speed of the action. Then ask them to try jogging on the spot, lifting the feet a little more and then moving around the hall. Check their spacing and encourage small steps with lots of changes of direction. Make a game of 'Statue stops' (jogging and stopping on command).

(10 mins) Floor work

Tell everyone to jump on the spot with squashy, light landings and then to try lifting their feet a bit higher off the ground.

Ask the children to try a different way of jumping, lifting their feet high (feet behind, in front or to the side). Encourage them to lift their feet a bit higher each time, with squashy landings, feet together.

Ask them to choose a different way of travelling on the feet – hopping, jumping, jogging – then encourage them to lift their feet further off the ground.

Tell the children to lie down and lift one foot high. This could be on their backs, sides or fronts. Ask them to lift part of their body off the floor to get their foot even higher. Encourage them to hold the shape for a count of three, then to lower themselves, turn over or move to another space to try another way of balancing with one foot or two feet high. (See Diagram 10.)

Ask them what they must remember to do before they move – look for spaces. Ask them to move on that part of their body to another space. Help them to become aware of which part of the body is touching the floor (backs, fronts, sides and so on) and how they can lift their foot higher. Use a few examples for demonstration and then encourage all the children to try either one of those ideas or a new way of their own.

Can they try travelling on hands and feet? Use demonstrations to illustrate two or three ways and ask everyone to try a different way. Check their spacing and that they are looking where they are going.

Diagram 10

Lifting feet high

Ask them to try some of the ways of balancing on hands and feet that they tried last week. *Can you stretch and lift that foot even more?*

14 **Apparatus work**
mins Refer to the apparatus notes and the apparatus plan on photocopiable page 124. In six groups, ask the children to try out some of the actions they have been trying this lesson on different parts of the apparatus. Insist on looking for spaces.

Advise everyone to use large parts of their bodies to make some still shapes on the apparatus. Can they lift one foot or both feet high? Look for different possibilities to use as demonstrations to suggest ideas to other children.

Ask them to try a way of travelling on their hands and feet to move around, towards or along the apparatus. Use demonstrations to illustrate two or three ways. Ask everyone to try a different way. Help them to use all parts of their apparatus and to space out well.

Ask them to find places on the apparatus where they can hold underneath it to lift one or both feet high (for example, planks or ladders).

To finish, let them select and practise their favourite actions.

3 **Cool-down**
mins Ask the children to jog slowly on the spot. Then tell them to lie down and relax and make their bodies go all floppy. Encourage them to stretch their arms and legs as wide as possible and relax again. Repeat several times.

Classroom review
Ask the children to describe some of the actions they tried, such as lifting their feet high as they moved or balanced. Ask: *What did you have to do to get your feet high?*

Assessing learning outcomes
Are the children understanding the task? Are they using different parts of their bodies? Are they spacing well and using all parts of the apparatus?

Lifting feet high

(30 mins) Can we think of more ways of lifting feet high?

Learning objectives
● Practise ways of travelling on feet with legs high.
● Practise ways of resting on parts of the body to lift feet high.
● Practise ways of lifting feet high on the apparatus.
● Select some favourite actions to link together.

Lesson organisation
Brief discussion in the classroom; individual warm-up and floor work; practise using apparatus in six groups; individual cool-down; teacher led classroom review.

Vocabulary
hopping
bunny jump
shoulder stand

What you need and preparation
You will need apparatus accessible for each of six groups; the apparatus plan on photocopiable page 124.

Discuss with the children the particular requirements for getting out and using apparatus (see Apparatus in the chapter introduction).

What to do

(4 mins) Warm-up
Ask the children to try little running steps on the spot, gradually lifting the feet more off the ground. Then ask them to try this moving around the hall. Encourage them to try lifting their feet up behind them.

Play a statue game. Check the children's spacing and encourage small steps and free movement with lots of changes of direction.

(10 mins) Floor work
Ask the class to hop on the spot (changing legs) and then to try with one foot held high. Now ask them to try moving around the hall, keeping in a space.

Tell the children to try another way of hopping with the foot held high off the ground (they could hold a knee up if necessary and then try without).

Encourage them to practise ways of travelling on both hands and one foot. Use demonstrations to illustrate two or three ways. Ask all the children to try a different way (tummy up or back up, for example).

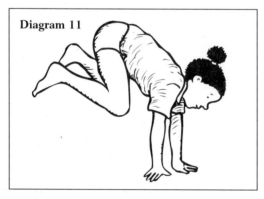

Diagram 11

Now ask them to place both hands flat on the floor, fingers forward, and to jump both feet a little off the ground (bunny jump). (See Diagram 11.) Encourage them to try a bit higher. Practise the bunny jump with squashy landings.

Ask the children to lie down. Tell them to try to lift both feet high. This could be on their backs, sides or fronts or on smaller parts such as shoulders. Use a few examples for demonstration and then encourage the children to try a new way of their own. If they are trying the shoulder stand, encourage them to support their hips with their hands.

To finish, ask the children to select and practise their favourite actions, then try to link a balancing action and a travelling action (with high feet).

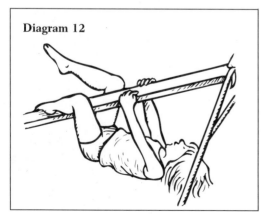

Diagram 12

(12 mins) Apparatus work
Referring to the apparatus notes and plan, ask the children in their six groups to get out their allocated apparatus. Ask them to rotate to the next arrangement of apparatus.

Ask them to try out on their apparatus some of the travelling actions they have just been trying. Encourage moving towards, away from, along, on and off or around the apparatus. Insist on looking for spaces and keeping moving. Can they lift one or both feet high?

Ask the class to use their bodies to move along, under or around parts of the apparatus. Encourage them to lift their legs high. (See Diagram 12.) Look for different possibilities to use as demonstrations to suggest ideas or to challenge other children.

Ask the children to use large parts of their bodies or their hands and feet to make a still shape with part of them on the floor and part of them on the apparatus. Prompt them with: *Can you try an upside down position?*

Ask them to select and practise their favourite actions, lifting their feet high, before carefully putting their apparatus away.

④ mins Cool-down

Ask the children to stand on one leg and keep still. Tell them to change legs and try again. Encourage them to count slowly to three and then put the lifted leg down. Ask them to try again, this time lifting the leg in a different position. How high can they lift their free leg?

Now ask the children to stand tall with their feet together on the floor, and to lower the body slowly to the ground, then relax and let their bodies go floppy.

Classroom review

Ask the children:
- How did you improve your actions today?
- Did you really stretch and lift your feet?
- What did you enjoy most?

Assessing learning outcomes

Are the children taking their weight safely on flat hands? Are they spacing well on the apparatus? Are they able to stretch their feet?

③⓪ mins How can we refine our high feet actions?

What you need and preparation

You will need apparatus accessible for each of six groups; the apparatus plan on photocopiable page 124.

In the classroom, talk about the special requirements for setting up apparatus (see the Apparatus section of the chapter introduction).

What to do

④ mins Warm-up

Ask the children to choose a way of travelling around the hall on their feet (hopping, jumping, jogging and so on).

Ask the children to skip around the hall. Then encourage stronger pushes to skip lifting the feet higher off the ground.

Play a non-elimination statues game using a choice of travelling action.

⑩ mins Floor work

Ask the children to practise ways of pushing with the arms to bunny jump. Encourage them to practise the bunny jump action on the spot with hands flat, and both feet lifting off the ground together. Can they do this moving along?

Now ask the children to lie down. Encourage them to try lying on a different part of their bodies from last time to lift both feet high. This could be on their backs, sides, fronts, bottoms or shoulders. Ask them all to try resting just on their shoulders to lift both feet high. See if they can support their hips with their hands. Can they stretch their feet towards the ceiling? (See Diagram 13 on page 22.)

Learning objectives
- Practise bunny jumps.
- Try a sideways roll and/or a teddy bear roll, lifting and lowering the feet.
- Select and try ways of lifting feet to make still shapes on the apparatus.
- Observe and comment constructively on a partner's performance.

Lesson organisation
Brief discussion in the classroom; individual warm-up; individual and paired floor work; practice using apparatus in six groups; individual cool-down; teacher-led classroom review in pairs.

Vocabulary
hopping
skipping
bunny jump
shoulder stand
teddy bear roll

Lifting feet high

Ask the children to lie in a long thin shape and to roll gently sideways. Then encourage them to try lifting and lowering one leg at a time as they do this.

Diagram 13

Ask them to try a teddy bear roll. Sitting with their legs wide apart, ask them to hold their legs or ankles. Then encourage them to tip gently to one side and roll down the side, across the back, lifting their feet high and keeping them wide apart until they are sitting facing the other direction. (See Diagram 14.)

Let the children practise any of their favourite ways of lifting one or two feet high, selecting a balance and a travelling action to link together.

In pairs, children could view each other's choices, say what they liked and suggest how they could be improved.

Diagram 14

12 **Apparatus work**
mins In their six groups, ask the children to get out their allocated apparatus. (See the notes on handling apparatus and the plan on photocopiable page 124.) Tell them to point and then move to their next piece of apparatus.

Ask the children to find places on the apparatus where they can make still shapes. Then ask them to try making the shapes with one foot or both feet high. Encourage good spacing and use of all parts of the apparatus, including the floor. This could involve sitting, lying, hanging or holding. Can they lower their feet (or foot) down to move to another space?

Ask the children to practise some of the travelling actions they have tried so far. Emphasise

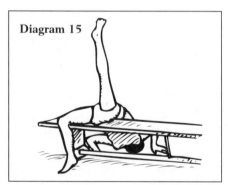

Diagram 15

towards, away from, along, over or around their group's new apparatus. Insist on looking for spaces and keeping moving. Ask: *Can you try hopping, jumping or bunny jumping?*

Ask the class to use parts of their body or their hands and feet to make a still shape with part of them on the apparatus and part of them on the floor. (See Diagram 15, for example.) Look for different possibilities to use as demonstrations to suggest ideas to other children. Encourage the children to maintain good control of their actions by lowering themselves down safely.

To finish, ask the children to select and practise two different actions lifting their feet high, and to practise them one after the other before carefully putting the apparatus away.

4 **Cool-down**
mins Ask the children to jump gently and then stop to stand on one leg. Tell them: *Try to hold a balance with one foot lifted as high as you can off the ground.* Encourage them to lower that foot, and try on the other foot. Repeat this and then ask them to relax.

Classroom review
Ask the children to think of two different ways of lifting their feet high that they tried on the apparatus today. Tell them to describe them to a partner.

Assessing learning outcomes
Are the children thinking about lifting their feet high? Are they using imaginative responses?

(30 mins) Can we practise ways of lifting and lowering?

What you need and preparation

You will need apparatus for six groups; the apparatus plan on photocopiable page 124.

Remind the children of the special requirements for getting out and using apparatus (see Apparatus on page 10).

What to do

(4 mins) Warm-up

Ask the children to hop on the spot (changing legs) and then to hop around the hall. Encourage a stronger hop, using their arms to hop higher and over a greater distance.

Ask the children to choose their favourite ways of travelling or jumping, lifting one foot or both feet high. Ask them to clarify what shape they are making with their legs.

(10 mins) Floor work

Ask the children to practise some travelling actions on hands and feet or other parts of the body, with one foot or both feet high.

Ask them to choose a still shape they have tried on hands and feet, lifting one foot high. Encourage them to practise lowering the leg and then the whole body down to the ground and then slowly rolling to a new space.

With hands flat, a shoulder-width apart, ask the children to hop and really stretch one leg high. Then ask them to try with the other leg. Can they scissor their legs in the air? Ask more able children to see if they can hold a balance with both legs high (a headstand).

Ask them to select and try ways of travelling and balancing with feet high and to start linking them together. Ensure that they use different parts of their bodies.

(12 mins) Apparatus work

In their six groups, ask the children get out their allocated apparatus. Tell them to point and then move to the next piece of apparatus they are to work on.

Ask the children to find different ways of lifting one or both feet and then lowering themselves on different parts of their apparatus.

Move on to help them to find places where they can bunny jump over or along parts of the apparatus (see Diagram 16).

Ask them to try travelling sideways over the bench or plank with legs wider apart (cart-wheel).

● Can they lean on parts of the apparatus (bars or benches) and lift one or both legs high?

● Can they hold underneath parts of the apparatus to lift their feet high?

● Can they hang on the ropes or hold on to the bars or against the box upside down?

Ask the children to choose and practise their favourite actions with high feet and then to practise different ways of linking them.

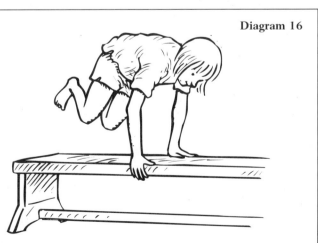

Diagram 16

Learning objectives
● Practise ways of lifting then lowering feet and moving into another action.
● Select and practise actions with one foot or both feet high, leading to a headstand.
● Practise and refine ways of travelling and balancing on different parts of the apparatus with feet high.
● Link actions to create a sequence on the floor and apparatus.

Lesson organisation
Brief classroom discussion; individual warm-up and floor work; apparatus practice in six groups; individual cool-down; teacher-led classroom review.

Vocabulary
scissor jump
headstand
bunny jump
cart-wheel

Lifting feet high

4 **Cool-down**
mins Ask the children to bunny jump on the spot, jumping feet from side to side, forwards and backwards. Tell them to tuck up small and then stretch out, lie down and relax.

Classroom review
Ask the children to think about the different actions that they chose or could choose to link together to make a sequence and to remember them for next week.

Assessing learning outcomes
Can the children perform a bunny jump? Are they selecting appropriate actions for their sequences?

30 How can we link and refine our high feet actions?
mins

What you need and preparation
You will need apparatus for six groups; a copy of the apparatus plan on photocopiable page 124.

Discuss with the children beforehand the special procedures for getting out the apparatus (see Apparatus on page 10).

What to do

4 **Warm-up**
mins Ask the children to choose one way of moving around the hall on their feet (for example hop, jump, jog, skip). Encourage them to keep moving and keep changing direction, always looking for spaces.

Ask the children: *Can you try a scissor kick in the air, getting both feet high, one after the other?* Encourage them to practise some different jumps.

12 **Floor work**
mins Let the children practise striding or leaping from one foot to the other. Encourage them to try getting higher off the ground.

Encourage them to practise still shapes on any part of the body. Practise lifting feet and lowering them down to move to try another balance.

Ask the children to try bunny jumps, moving sideways or backwards. Emphasise looking before moving. Encourage them to try a sideways cart-wheeling action, emphasising the even rhythm, 1, 2, 3, 4 (see Diagram 17).

Ask them to select and practise their favourite travelling and balancing actions with both feet high and to link them together to make a sequence on the floor. Encourage them to show you their start and finish positions. Ask them to check that they have included a jump and at least two different balances.

12 **Apparatus work**
mins In their six groups, ask the children get out their allocated apparatus. Tell them to point and then move to the apparatus they are to work on.

Ask them to select and practise their favourite actions and to link them together to make a sequence on the apparatus.

Learning objectives
● Practise ways of lifting feet high.
● Explore ways of bunny jumping in different directions.
● Practise and refine ways of lifting feet high to create a sequence on the floor and apparatus.

Lesson organisation
Brief classroom discussion; individual warm-up; individual floor work; apparatus work in groups; individual cool-down; teacher-led classroom review.

Vocabulary
scissor kick
striding
leaping
bunny jump
cart-wheel
bottom balance

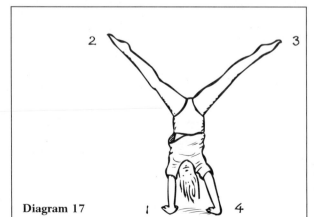
Diagram 17

2   3
I   4

Remind them to include two still balances and two travelling actions with high feet. Encourage them to practise ways of joining them together smoothly, making the end of one movement become the beginning of the next.

Watch half the class perform their high feet sequences, and then swap over. Ask all the children to try their individual sequences once more before putting the apparatus away carefully.

2 mins Cool-down

Ask the children to jog slowly on the spot. Then tell them to sit down and rest on both hands, just behind their bottom, lifting both feet high (bottom balance). Ask them to lower their legs down, turn over and let the whole body relax.

Classroom review

Ask the children to discuss what they liked about some of the sequences they observed and offer suggestions for improvement.

Assessing learning outcomes

Can the children link their chosen actions into a sequence? Can they describe their actions? Can they say what they liked and what could be improved?

Linking actions: bridging, sliding and jumping

The focus for this series of lessons will develop children's experience of linking actions. A simple sequence can be likened to a sentence of movements with a beginning, middle and end. It will enable them to choose movements with which they are confident and select and develop their own ideas within the context of the task set.

Children will have the opportunity to practise and consolidate some movements as they join them together and repeat them. This will develop their movement memory (planning, deciding and remembering the order of actions) and give them additional opportunities for co-ordination and control as they try different ways of linking them. Stamina and strength should also develop as the children repeat and practise different movement combinations.

It is helpful if there is a specific focus for the choice of actions. The focus on bridging will help to develop and broaden children's experience of balance by helping them to consider still shapes (wide and narrow; high and low) and different aspects of stability and the span or height of their bridges. The focus on sliding and jumping will develop specific aspects of travelling that will help them link their actions.

It is presumed that children will have had a variety of experiences of different ways of travelling and balancing on different parts of the body during Key Stage 1 and that they are developing more control of their actions. Although most children will have had some experience of handling apparatus, they will need to be taught how to do this safely.

The unit is divided into six sessions allowing 30–40 minutes of activity per session. Each session will involve both floor work and apparatus work, but ideas can be modified to suit individual school contexts. The class can be divided into six groups (approximately five per group) to ensure good spacing and fair turns on each group of apparatus.

The suggested apparatus plan on photocopiable page 125 is meant as a guide only, and it shows how the groups could rotate between apparatus.

Because many of the actions involve sliding on the body it is important that the floor and the apparatus are clean, smooth and in good condition.

UNIT: Linking actions: bridging, sliding and jumping

Enquiry questions	Learning objectives	Teaching activities	Learning outcomes
Can we make bridges with our bodies?	• Practise and refine ways of travelling on feet. • Explore ways of sliding, using legs and arms to assist. • Explore ways of bridging, using hands and feet. • Try ways of sliding and bridging to link together on the floor. • Practise handling benches and mats safely.	Warm-up: jogging on the spot, gradually lifting feet higher and varying speed; noticing changes to heartbeat and breathing; practising travelling on feet. Floor work: practising travelling on feet and linking; practising balancing; making bridges; sliding; sliding, pushing up into a bridge. Apparatus work: travelling on feet or hands using apparatus; sliding actions on the floor; making still shapes on or against the bench; making a bridge, part on the bench, part on the floor; practising favourite bridges. Cool-down: lying down, relaxing and tensing muscles.	Children: • are inventive with their actions • think of different ways they can make bridges • use the space well
Which parts of the body can we use to make bridges?	• Practise ways of jumping and landing. • Explore ways of bridging, using the body on the floor and apparatus. • Try ways of sliding and jumping, using the apparatus. • Begin to link actions on the floor and apparatus.	Warm-up: jumping on the spot and making a pattern of jumps on the spot; practising jumping from one foot to two feet; linking two jumps with a jogging action. Floor work: practising jumping from two feet to two feet, then lower to sitting then lying; practising jumping with different shapes; sliding on different parts of the body; joining jumping and sliding; practising different shaped bridges on hands and feet and other parts. Apparatus work: jumping and sliding using apparatus; practising jumping, landing and sliding; practising bridges on parts of the apparatus. Cool-down: lying down and relaxing; stretching wide and relaxing.	• understand making bridges • hold balances still for the count of three • handle apparatus safely
How can we refine ways of bridging, sliding and jumping?	• Refine the shape of jumps. • Practise ways of bridging using different parts of the body. • Refine ways of sliding • Try some ways of rolling. • Explore ways of using different parts of the apparatus to make bridges. • Link actions on the floor and apparatus.	Warm-up: running on the spot, alternating lifting knees and heels; playing 'statue stops'; making shapes in pairs. Floor work: practising jumping from two feet to two feet in different shapes; moving on the body to another space to make a bridge; linking actions together smoothly. Apparatus work: trying sliding actions using apparatus; making bridges on the apparatus; linking together bridging and travelling actions. Cool-down: with hands flat on the floor, jumping feet forwards and backwards; relaxing.	• think how they can refine their actions • space well and using different parts of their apparatus

UNIT: Linking actions: bridging, sliding and jumping

Enquiry questions	Learning objectives	Teaching activities	Learning outcomes
Can we lower the bridges we make with our bodies?	● Practise jumping with hands and feet (bunny jump, cat spring). ● Practise lowering bridges and sliding or rolling to a new space on the floor and on the apparatus. ● Try different ways of linking actions together on the floor and on the apparatus. ● Think how actions can be linked together smoothly.	Warm-up: skipping on the spot and around the space; playing 'Statue stops'. Floor work: practising running and leaping; practising travelling on hands and feet; practising making bridges using different parts of the body; practising three bridges using hands and feet. Apparatus work: trying ways of sliding, rolling or jumping using the apparatus; practising making strong bridges; practising linking bridges and travelling actions. Cool-down: trying bottom balances; stretching and relaxing.	● understand and demonstrate linking actions ● begin to do this smoothly
Can we put bridging actions into a sequence?	● Practise ways of jumping, landing and linking other actions. ● Select and practise different bridging actions to put into a sequence. ● Practise ways of linking actions on the apparatus.	Warm-up: hopping on the spot and around the space; practising ways of jumping. Floor work: practising different bridge shapes; selecting ways of sliding or rolling; practising travelling and then pushing up into the bridge, then lowering down; practising jumping, landing and then another action, and linking these together. Apparatus work: practising sliding, rolling or jumping from one part of the apparatus to another; practising bridging actions against the apparatus; linking actions together on the apparatus. Cool-down: practising a bottom balance lift; lying down; stretching; relaxing.	● select appropriate actions for their sequences ● include a sliding, a jumping and at least two bridging actions
How can we refine our sequences?	● Select, practise and refine ways of bridging, jumping and sliding to create a sequence on the floor and apparatus. ● Evaluate own and other's sequences of linked actions.	Warm-up: moving on the feet, changing direction; following a partner's footsteps. Floor work: selecting and practising leaps and jumps; practising bridges, lowering down into a travelling action; linking bridging and travelling actions to make a sequence with start and finish positions. Apparatus work: linking together bridging and travelling actions into a sequence on the apparatus. Cool-down: doing press ups on all fours; relaxing.	● demonstrate linking their chosen actions into a sequence ● choose starting and finishing positions ● link actions together smoothly.

Cross-curricular links
Design and technology / science: understanding structures and stability; bridge span.
Maths: sequencing actions.
English: linking actions like a sentence with a beginning, middle and end.

Resources
Apparatus for six groups; the apparatus plan on photocopiable page 125.

Can we make bridges with our bodies?

What you need and preparation

You will need one bench or box-top and mat for each of six groups (approximately five children per group).

In the classroom, discuss bridges with the children. Ask them what sort of bridges they have seen. Talk about safety and ask: *What special behaviour is required for getting to the hall and doing PE?* (See Apparatus on page 10).

What to do

6 mins Warm-up

Ensure everyone is well spaced to start the warm-up.

Ask the children to jog on the spot and encourage light footwork, checking that there is good articulation of their ankles. Start with the toes hardly leaving the floor then gradually encourage the children to lift their feet a little higher off the ground (vary the action – feet high, feet hardly leaving the ground).

Now tell them to jog forwards in and out all over the hall, looking for spaces. Ask them to jog in another direction and to think about what they need to remember when they are going backwards. (To be aware of where they are going.) Encourage the use of other directions (sideways or diagonally). Observe the responses and suggest everyone tries jogging in two directions.

Encourage the children to increase the speed of the jogging action and to lift their knees. This will raise the pulse, so ask them what they are noticing about their heartbeat and breathing.

Ask them to think of and practise a different way of travelling on their feet (for example hopping or jumping) while moving around the hall looking for spaces.

12 mins Floor work

Ask the children to think of and practise two or three ways of travelling on their hands and feet (walking on all fours, bunny jumping), making sure they are looking where they are going. Encourage them to choose two to link together. Can they practise going smoothly from one to the other?

In their own space, ask them to try ways they could make still, strong, balanced shapes. Select some children to demonstrate bridges then help everyone to explore other possible ways of making bridges. Encourage them to use different parts of their bodies (hands and feet, knees and one hand). Look for and encourage original ideas.

Choose two or three more children to demonstrate and then ask all the children to try one of those or other new ways.

Choose two examples of bridges using hands and feet to show the class and then ask all the children to try just using their hands and their feet (tummy uppermost or back uppermost – see Diagram 18; different combinations of hands and feet). Emphasise usings strong arms and flat hands to support the body. Can they think of other ways they can make a strong, stable bridge?

Ask them to think about the shape of their bridge and to see if they can make a narrow or wide one. Let them try several ways.

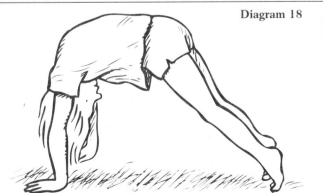

Diagram 18

Learning objectives

- Practise and refine ways of travelling on feet.
- Explore ways of sliding, using legs and arms to assist.
- Explore ways of bridging, using hands and feet.
- Try ways of sliding and bridging to link together on the floor.
- Practise handling benches and mats safely.

Lesson organisation

Classroom discussion; individual warm-up and floor work; practice using benches or box-tops in six groups; individual cool-down; teacher-led classroom review.

Vocabulary

stability
base
body tension
balance
diagonally
bridge span

Linking actions

Practise lying down and pushing up into that shape. Encourage the children to keep body shape and tension. Challenge them by asking if they can raise their bridge a bit more before lowering it to lie down.

On backs, sides or tummies, ask them to slide themselves along. Use demonstrations to illustrate two or three ways. Ask everyone to think about whether they used their hands or their feet to move along. Ask them to try other ways and then to choose a favourite way to practise.

Ask them to show you this sliding action and then to think of ways they could push themselves up into a bridge. Encourage them to try several ways they could do this.

⑩ mins Apparatus work

With the children in their six groups, teach each group how to get out a bench or box-top and a mat, and where to put them.

Ask them to try a way of travelling on their feet or hands and feet to move towards, away from, along or around the bench. Insist on looking for spaces and keeping moving. Use demonstrations to illustrate two or three ways. Ask all the children to try several more ways.

Now let them try out some of the sliding actions they tried earlier along the bench, along the floor or even under the bench.

Ask everyone to use their hands and their feet to make a still shape on the floor or mat, or on or against the bench. Can they make a bridge with their bodies?

Ask them to try to make a bridge with part of them on the bench and part of them on the floor (or part on mat, part on floor). Look for different possibilities to use as demonstrations to suggest ideas to other children.

Let the children practise their favourite bridges. Encourage them to slide to a new space to make another bridge, before asking the groups to carefully put their apparatus away.

② mins Cool-down

Ask the children to lie down and relax and make their bodies go all floppy. Tell them to pull all their muscles tight and then relax again. Repeat the sequence.

Classroom review

Encourage the children to describe some of the bridges they tried today. Ask:
● What parts of the body did you use?
● Did you make the bridges strong and firm?
● What helped you to do this?

Assessing learning outcomes

Are the children being inventive with their actions? Do they think of different ways they can make bridges? Do they use the space well?

(30 mins) Which parts of the body can we use to make bridges?

What you need and preparation

Make sure that apparatus for six groups is ready around the sides of the hall. You will also need the apparatus plan on photocopiable page 125.

In the classroom, go through the special requirements for handling and using apparatus (see Apparatus on page 10).

What to do

(6 mins) Warm-up

Ask the children to jump on the spot with light, springy landings. Encourage them to have flexible feet and gradually lift them further off the ground. Tell them to move from side to side and then forwards and backwards, and then to make a pattern of jumps.

Ask them to try different ways of jumping as they move around the hall. Check their spacing and encourage them to use soft landings.

Ask the children to choose one of their ways for everyone to practise or ask them all to try jumping from one foot to land on two feet. Practise this several times, asking them how they could improve their jump. (Use their arms, squashy landings and so on.)

Tell them to choose two of the jumps to link together with a jogging action in between. Encourage them to land and then immediately continue moving.

(10 mins) Floor work

On the spot, ask the children to practise jumping from two feet to two feet with soft, squashy landings. Repeat, asking them to lower themselves gently down into sitting then lying positions. Emphasise bending the hips, knees and ankles to absorb the forces on landing.

Ask the children to practise jumping, asking them what different shapes they can make in the air.

Ask them to lie down (on their backs, sides or fronts) and to slide on that part of their body to another space. Help them to become aware of which part of the body is touching the floor and then, more importantly, which part they are using most to move themselves along.

Encourage them to link a jumping and a sliding action.

Now ask them to try some of the bridges they made on hands and feet in the last lesson and then to think about the different shapes they could make. Select some to demonstrate a narrow or wide one. Teach or remind them of the press up or front support position, then ask them to turn over and to try with their tummies uppermost. Emphasise thin shapes then encourage them to try with their hands and feet wide apart.

Diagram 19

Ask them to try bridges using other parts of their bodies (shoulders and feet, elbows and knees – see Diagram 19). Use a few examples for demonstration and then encourage the children to try one of those ideas or a new way of their own. It could be that two children are on their backs or shoulders but are using two feet or one foot. Encourage them to hold the balance or bridge for a count of three.

In pairs, children could show each other the ways they have found.

Learning objectives
● Practise ways of jumping and landing.
● Explore ways of bridging, using the body on the floor and apparatus.
● Try ways of sliding and jumping using the apparatus.
● Begin to link actions on the floor and apparatus.

Lesson organisation
Brief classroom discussion; individual warm-up; floor work individually and in pairs; apparatus practice in six groups; individual cool-down; teacher-led classroom review.

Vocabulary
springy landings
flexible feet
absorb forces

Linking actions

 Apparatus work
12 mins In their six groups, tell the children to get out their allocated apparatus, according to the apparatus plan on photocopiable page 125.

Ask them to try out some of the jumping and sliding actions they have tried this lesson, towards, away from, along or around their group's apparatus. Insist on looking for spaces and keeping moving. Encourage them to try both actions.

Advise them to use lower parts of their apparatus where they can practise jumping and landing and then to slide along the floor to a new space.

Ask the children to use their bodies to make a bridge on parts of the apparatus. Ask one or two children to demonstrate different possibilities to suggest ideas or challenge the rest of the class. Advise everyone to space out to use different parts of their apparatus.

Ask the children to select and practise their favourite bridging actions.

Check before they put their apparatus away that they know which apparatus to rotate to next week. Remind them that they will continue to get out and put away this apparatus because they will know what to use and where to put it.

 Cool-down
2 mins Ask the children to lie down and relax and make the body go all floppy. Encourage them to stretch their arms and legs as wide as possible and relax again. Repeat this stretch and relax instruction several times.

Classroom review
Encourage the children to describe some of the actions they tried today. Which ways did they find of making bridges on their apparatus?

Assessing learning outcomes
Do the children understand making bridges? Can they hold the balances still for the count of three? Are they handling apparatus safely?

30 mins How can we refine ways of bridging, sliding and jumping?

Learning objectives
● Refine the shapes of jumps.
● Practise ways of bridging using different parts of the body.
● Refine ways of sliding.
● Try some ways of rolling.
● Explore ways of using different parts of the apparatus to make bridges.
● Link actions on the floor and apparatus.

Lesson organisation
Brief discussion in the classroom; warm-up individually and in pairs; individual floor work; apparatus practice in six groups; individual cool-down; teacher-led classroom review.

What you need and preparation
You will need apparatus ready around the sides of the hall for six groups (approximately five children per group); the apparatus plan on photocopiable page 125.

Discuss with children in the classroom the special requirements for getting out the apparatus (see Apparatus on page 10).

What to do
 Warm-up
6 mins To start, tell the children to try little running steps on the spot, then to lift their knees gradually higher as they do so. Then ask them to try this while they move around the hall. Challenge them to try it with their heels up behind them. Check their spacing and encourage them to take small steps with free movement with lots of changes of direction. Alternate between knees high in front to heels high behind.

Play a non-elimination statue game. On your *Stop* signal, the children should make and hold a still shape.

Linking actions

Now ask the children to find a partner. One of them makes a long, thin, still shape on all fours (front or back support). Their partner jumps over their feet and slides under their middle five times. Then change over to repeat.

(10 mins) Floor work
Ask the children to practise jumping from two feet to two feet, pushing with their legs and swinging their arms to assist jumping.

Encourage them to practise jumping, asking them to think about the different shapes they could make in the air. Ask them to choose two shapes they want to practise and improve. Encourage clarity of shape.

Then ask the children to lie down, using a different part of their body this time (bottoms, sides or fronts). Ask them to move on that part of their body to another space and then to push up onto a smaller part to make a bridge (on shoulders – see Diagram 20 – or elbows). Explore and practise several ways. Use a few examples for demonstration and then encourage them all to try other ways of making bridges. Ask them:

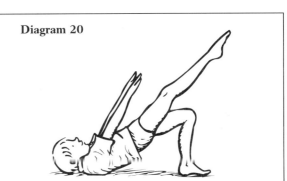
Diagram 20

● Can you try on your sides?
● Can you make a bridge using just your feet?
● Can it be a high or a low bridge?

Ask them to try to link some of those actions together – a jump, land, lie and slide along and then push up into a bridge.

Individually, ask them to think how they could link the actions together more smoothly and try to practise that (for example by making the end of one action the beginning of the next).

(12 mins) Apparatus work
In their six groups, ask the children get out their allocated apparatus. Once all the apparatus is out, ask the children to point and then move to the next apparatus.

Ask the children to try out some of the sliding actions they have tried so far, towards, away from, along or around their group's new apparatus. Insist on looking for spaces and keeping moving. Ask them to try different ways they can make bridges on this apparatus.

Let the children select examples to practise. Look for different possibilities and ask some children to demonstrate. Encourage everyone to use controlled actions.

See if everyone can link together two or three different actions (for example sliding and bridging or jumping, sliding and bridging).

Tell them to practise their ideas on the next arrangement of apparatus, before asking them to put their apparatus away carefully.

(2 mins) Cool-down
Placing their hands flat on the floor, ask the children to push with their arms straight and to jump their feet forwards and backwards. Encourage everyone to finish in the front support position and lower their bodies slowly to the ground, then relax and let their bodies go floppy.

Classroom review
Ask the children: *How did you improve your actions? What did you enjoy most in this lesson?*

Assessing learning outcomes
Are the children thinking how they could refine their actions? Are they spacing well and using different parts of their apparatus?

Linking actions

30 mins Can we lower the bridges we make with our bodies?

What you need and preparation

Have apparatus for six groups of about five children ready around the sides of the hall. You will also need the apparatus plan on photocopiable page 131.

Remind the children beforehand of the special requirements for getting out and working on apparatus.

What to do

5 mins Warm-up

Ask the children to skip on the spot and then around the hall using all the space. Encourage lifting feet higher off the ground. Repeat using different directions.

Use skipping to play a statues game, asking the children to hold a still shape on your *Stop* signal.

10 mins Floor work

Ask the children to practise running and leaping (see Diagram 21) from one foot to the other. Encourage them to try taking off and landing with the other foot too. Use any lines on the floor or imaginary puddles to jump over. Encourage sinking into steps to continue running.

Now let them practise different ways of travelling on hands and feet (bunny jump or cat spring, for example). Emphasise a pounce onto flat hands, pushing with the legs.

Ask the children to make bridges using different parts of their bodies. Practise several ways then ask:

● Can you use your feet and two other parts?
● What about your feet and one other part?
● Can you use other small parts (hand, foot and head, knee and hand)?

Ask them to remember and make three different bridges using just their hands and feet. Look at different examples to illustrate stability. Ask the class whether it is easier to use the hand and the foot

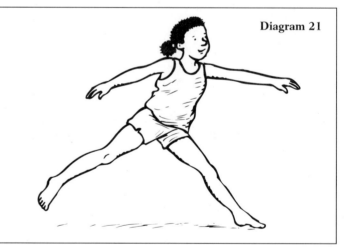

Diagram 21

on the same side of the body or the hand and foot on different sides. Ask for demonstrations to illustrate different ways.

Let everyone choose one bridge, then lower themselves down onto their backs or fronts and to slide along or turn over and roll sideways into a new space as smoothly as they can. Ask them to try different ways of lowering and moving along. Use the children's ideas to demonstrate and to suggest actions to others.

In pairs, ask the children to show each other their chosen movements and suggest how they could be improved.

12 mins Apparatus work
In their six groups, ask the children to get out their allocated apparatus and then to rotate to the next apparatus they are to use.

Ask the children to try out some of the sliding, rolling or jumping actions they have tried so far, towards, away from, along or around their group's new apparatus. Insist on looking for spaces and keeping moving.

Tell them to find different places on the apparatus where they can make strong bridges. Encourage good spacing and use of all parts of the apparatus, including the floor. Select examples to practise. Look for original ideas for demonstration. Ask others to practise these or other ideas. Emphasise stillness, holding the bridge for the count of three and then lowering down to move or slide to another part of the apparatus to make another bridge.

Ask them to find places on their apparatus where they can:
● travel on their bodies (slide or roll) and then make a bridge
● travel using hands and feet and then make a bridge.

Encourage them to select and practise ways of linking these actions on the apparatus.

Get them to repeat this on the next arrangement of apparatus, before asking the groups to carefully put their apparatus away.

2 mins Cool-down
Ask the children to sit with their feet stretched out in front of them. With their hands flat on the floor just behind their bottoms (shoulder-width apart), ask them to lift and then lower both legs and to lift and then lower their hips. Then invite them to lie down and relax.

Classroom review
Ask the children to think of three different ways that they made bridges on the apparatus today and to describe them to a partner.

Assessing learning outcomes
Do the children understand and can they demonstrate the linking actions? Are they beginning to do this smoothly?

30 mins Can we put bridging actions into a sequence?

What you need and preparation
You will need apparatus for six groups (approximately five children per group); the apparatus plan on photocopiable page 125.

Remind the children in the classroom of the important requirements for getting out their apparatus (see Apparatus on page 10).

What to do
4 mins Warm-up
Ask the children to hop on the spot and then to swap legs and repeat. Tell them then to hop around the hall. Encourage hopping in different directions.

Ask them to think of some other ways of jumping and to practise them (for example two feet or one foot take off or landing).

Encourage them to practise ways of leaping, landing and running to a new space. Encourage soft landings, then emphasise keeping their heads up and trying to stretch out in the air.

Learning objectives
● Practise ways of jumping, landing and linking other actions.
● Select and practise bridging actions to put into a sequence.
● Practise ways of linking actions on the apparatus.

Lesson organisation
Brief classroom discussion; individual warm-up and floor work; apparatus practice in six groups; teacher-led classroom review in pairs.

Linking actions

Vocabulary
bridging
refining
sequence

8 mins **Floor work**

Let the children practise some of their favourite bridge shapes. Encourage them to hold the bridge for a count of three before moving on to try a different one. Ask them if they can think of some new ways of making bridges. *Can you make a bridge with more than one arch? Can you make a bridge with a special shape?*

Ask the children to choose their favourite ways of sliding or rolling themselves along. Advise them to clarify what shape they are making with their legs as they move.

Tell them to practise moving and then pushing up into the bridge, holding the shape, then slowly lowering themselves down.

Ask them to practise ways of jumping, landing and adding another action (such as land then bunny jump; land, lower and slide; land and make a bridge).

Encourage them to think of and try different ways of linking these actions together. Remind them to think about which action they want to begin with and which to end with.

16 mins **Apparatus work**

In their six groups, ask the children to get out their allocated apparatus and then to rotate to the next apparatus.

Ask them to find different places on the apparatus where they can make bridges. Emphasise still balances, and see if they can hold them for a count of three.

Ask the children to find different ways of sliding, rolling or jumping on the floor as they move from one part of the apparatus to another.

Now ask them to find places where they can jump to get on or off the apparatus – using their hands and feet.

Finally, let them choose their favourite bridging actions on or against different parts of their apparatus, to practise them and link them together. Have they chosen a sliding or rolling action and a hands-and-feet jumping action to link their bridges together?

Ask them to repeat these tasks on the next arrangement of apparatus before carefully putting away their group's apparatus.

2 mins **Cool-down**

Ask the children to sit with their feet wide apart and toes stretched. As in the previous lesson, ask them to place their hands behind their bottoms (fingers forward) and to lift and then lower the legs, and then to lift and lower the hips.

Ask them to lie down and stretch out in a long, thin shape and then relax.

Classroom review

Ask the children to think about the different actions that they chose or could choose to link together to make a sequence and to remember them for next week. Encourage them to describe these actions to a partner and to think how they might improve them.

Assessing learning outcomes

Are the children selecting appropriate actions for their sequence? Are they including a sliding, a jumping and at least two bridging actions?

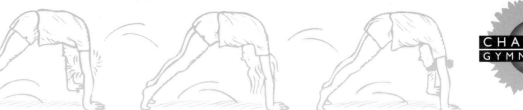

30 mins How can we refine our sequences?

What you need and preparation
You will need apparatus ready around the sides of the hall for six groups; the apparatus plan on photocopiable page 125.

In the classroom before going to the hall, remind the children of the requirements for setting out and using apparatus (see Apparatus on page 10).

What to do

4 mins Warm-up
Ask the children to choose and show you one way of moving around the hall on their feet (for example hop, jump, jog or skip). Encourage them to keep moving and keep changing direction, always looking for spaces.

Play 'Following footsteps'. In pairs, ask one child to lead, using some of the actions just practised, and their partner to follow in their footsteps as carefully as they can. Make sure they take turns to lead and follow.

8 mins Floor work
Let the children practise their favourite jumps (perhaps taking off on two feet and landing on two feet; one foot to two feet or leap) and then ask them all to practise leaping from one foot to the other. Ask them to practise jumping using hands and feet.

Encourage the children to practise their favourite or new bridges, lowering down into a sliding action or turning or rolling over into a new bridge. Allow them to select and practise their favourite two or three bridging actions and to link them together. Can they use some of the travelling actions (sliding or jumping) they have been practising to make a sequence on the floor? Encourage held start and finish positions and smooth joins between actions.

In pairs, ask the children to show their sequences and to comment on each other's work.

16 mins Apparatus work
In their six groups, ask the children to get out their allocated apparatus and then to move as a group to their next apparatus.

Let them select and practise their favourite bridging actions and ask them to link them together to make a sequence on the apparatus.

Watch three of the groups perform their linked sequences showing bridging actions, then the other groups. Finally, ask everyone to carefully put away their group's apparatus.

2 mins Cool-down
Ask the children to get into the press up position and to lower the body down slowly to the ground. Tell them to push up again and turn over and lower the body to the ground. Then ask them to let the whole body relax.

Classroom review
Ask the children to say what they liked about the ways in which the actions were joined together in some of the sequences they observed.

Assessing learning outcomes
Can the children demonstrate linking their chosen actions into a sequence? Can they choose starting and finishing positions? Can they link the actions together smoothly?

Learning objectives
● Select, practise and refine ways of bridging, jumping and sliding to create a sequence on the floor and apparatus.
● Evaluate own and other's sequences of linked actions.

Lesson organisation
Brief classroom discussion; individual and paired warm-up and floor work; apparatus practice in six groups; teacher-led classroom review.

Vocabulary
bridging
lowering

Follow-up activity
To extend this theme, ask the children to work in pairs. One of them can then make a bridge and the other one slide through or around to then make a bridge.

CHAPTER 2

Dance

Dance, like language, is present in all cultures, and this chapter contains suggestions to enable every child to develop and express their ideas in movement. Emphasis is placed on encouraging children to move with confidence, often starting with actions that are familiar and that they all can do, then developing the imaginative, creative and expressive aspects of each activity.

Most children love to move to music and will gradually become more aware of and able to respond to the rhythmic qualities of dance. The appreciation and use of sounds, music and rhythms is an integral part of this process. With varied stimuli and the use of contrasting experiences, children can be helped to clarify and refine their ideas and actions, keeping in time with different types of accompaniment. During Key Stage 1, children will have had the opportunity to perform basic skills (travelling, making shapes, being still and gesturing) in a creative dance context.

The warm-up and preparation aspects include listening and responding to the beat, using individual parts of the body to develop body awareness as well as warming up the body and using different types of travelling step.

Situations are then suggested to provide a framework for children's ideas and movements. Highlighting contrasting qualities, for example strong and light; fast and slow; high and low; curving and straight; large and small, will help children to raise their awareness of movement and clarify their actions. By using a variety of contexts and words such as *heave* or *float* to evoke particular qualities in their actions, children will begin to understand words through their actions and equally refine their actions through the use of words.

Within a clear framework suggested by each topic, the children will need time to explore and practise ideas to develop their creativity, to express themselves and sense the satisfaction from the composition of their own unique movement phrases. It is this process of exploring, creating and then linking actions which is most important and, although there are many opportunities to share and observe each other's ideas, performing to the rest of the group is not necessary at every draft stage.

Describing and discussing what they and others have done will help to develop their ability to appreciate and improve the quality of their work, but the main emphasis must be on practical participation and involvement. Some music pieces have been suggested, but percussion or the use of sounds or words themselves will be more readily available often be a simpler and more immediate way to support children with their dance movements.

The topics chosen for this chapter have been selected to provide examples of the use of everyday working actions and a story as stimuli for dance. The opportunities they provide will encourage children to respond in ways that will challenge them physically, imaginatively and intellectually and help them to access their feelings. Developing body actions into dance-like phrases will help to expand and enrich their experiences.

Sailors

This unit uses a historical topic to support and enrich movement possibilities. Key actions from working on board one of the tea clippers like the *Cutty Sark* provide the focus for the dance possibilities in this unit.

Dinosaurs and All That Rubbish

The use of the story of *Dinosaurs and All That Rubbish* by Michael Foreman (Puffin Books) provides opportunities to develop and explore a variety of working actions alongside movements with contrasting qualities. Creating a small-group celebratory dance will introduce children to elements of country dance, and the theme will help to provide a context for discussion of important environmental issues.

Sailors

The observation of people at work could be the focus for a series of lessons. It would help children to observe, appreciate the rhythm and the qualities of working actions.

This unit consists of six sessions allowing 30–40 minutes of activity per session. The class will create, perform, think about and appreciate dances individually, in pairs, in groups or as a whole class.

Knowledge and experience of the game 'Port and starboard' (detailed on photocopiable page 126) will be helpful as a basic starting point or stimulus for this series of lessons.

Research about the sort of jobs sailors did on tea clippers like the *Cutty Sark* would enable children to understand the hazardous and hard work involved on the tall sailing ships. It would also help them to analyse the movements (time and motion study) involved and to refine and combine them to create a group or class dance.

A small section of the introduction in the video *Pocahontas*, which portrays cartoon characters working on a sailing ship, might be a starting point for discussion.

In dance lessons, the actions can start from mime and develop into more rhythmic and exaggerated phrases of movement to music. Development stages of the phrases might be:

● Develop the rhythm of the action. For example, scrubbing the deck – push and pull and push and pull and dip in the bucket.

● Clarify the action – shape of hand, size and type of tool used, weight of implement and so on.

● Exaggerate the action – make it larger than life, use the whole body.

● Clarify the rhythm – preparation, action and recovery.

● Develop a phrase of actions. For example, pulling in the anchor – pull and pull and pull and rest; climb the rigging – climb and climb and climb and look.

● Repeat the phrases two or three times. Can the action be done in another way – with the other hand, in another position?

● Clarify the quality. Is it very hard work? Which parts of the action are very strong? Which are relaxed?

● Combine phrases of movement.

● Try an action with a partner or in a group.

These guidelines can be adapted to a number of topics that include working actions. Other dance activities could include sessions on:

● working on a building site

● cleaning windows or car washing

● cutting, threading and sewing

● harvest time

● coal mining

● Negro spirituals

● the slave trade.

The first suggestion, working on a building site, could be worked through as follows:

● Observe people working on a building site and think about the different jobs that they do. Think about some that need very strong movements and those that need very careful, precise movements.

● What are the different jobs that need to be done on a building site? Try miming some of them. Focus on posture, shape, place, action, force, timing, rhythm emphasis.

● Develop the motif – enlarge and exaggerate. Can your partner tell what you are doing?

● Develop the rhythm of the action, for example using an axe – chop and lift over shoulder, chop and lift over shoulder.

● Clarify the action – shape of hand, size and type of tool used, weight of implement and so on.

● Exaggerate the action – make it larger than life, use the whole body.

● Clarify the rhythm – preparation, action and recovery.

● Develop a phrase of actions – pull and pull and pull and rest; bang and bang and bang and move; lift and swing, lift and swing and wipe the brow.

● Repeat the phrases two or three times. Can the action be done in another way – with the other hand, in another position?

● Clarify the quality. Is it very hard work? Which parts of the action are very strong? Which are relaxed?

● Combine phrases of movement.

● Try an action with a partner or in a group.

UNIT: Sailors

Enquiry questions	Learning objectives	Teaching activities	Learning outcomes
What work did sailors do on the tall ships?	● Listen, travel and create step patterns to the music of the hornpipe. ● Learn a basic hornpipe step and create one. ● Practise some simple working action phrases. ● Begin to use different levels and directions in working actions. ● Create a simple pattern of dance phrases in twos.	Warm-up: tapping one foot then the other in time to the music; making a pattern of taps; walking in time with the beat, using different directions and pathways; making up a step pattern to the hornpipe music. Development: practising hornpipe ideas; practising a hornpipe phrase – moving to the right and left, adding an arm action; linking travelling action and hornpipe step; trying out different jobs on board ship; trying a rowing action; trying ideas for 'on the look out'; practising stretch and look phrase. Dance: practising working actions in pairs. Cool-down: walking, swinging arms strongly then gently; repeating step, stretch and look phrase.	Children: ● respond to and move in time with music ● contribute and develop their own ideas for hornpipe and working actions
Can we practise the hornpipe?	● Practise side-step to the hornpipe. ● Refine other hornpipe ideas. ● Practise other working action phrases. ● Create and practise a pattern of dance phrases in twos.	Warm-up: bouncing on the spot, practising the side-step to hornpipe music; trying a different hornpipe step. Development: practising own hornpipe step individually and in pairs; combining hornpipe steps in a sequence; adding travelling action; practising other working actions in a rhythmic phrase; trying climbing the rigging and scrubbing the decks. Dance: choosing and practising a working action in pairs; combining the hornpipe with a working action. Cool-down: skipping, slowing to a halt; stretching and looking.	● refine their movements for the hornpipe ● develop working actions into rhythmic phrases
What other jobs do sailors do on board ship?	● Practise different pathways and changing direction while walking to a beat. ● Revise and practise a hornpipe sequence. ● Practise other working action phrases. ● Create and practise a pattern of working action dance phrases.	Warm-up: practising walking using curving pathways then slip change of step to the hornpipe music; practising and refining hornpipe in pairs. Development: practising sewing the nets, developing and repeating a phrase; practising hauling in the anchor in a rhythmic phrase; practising turning the winch individually and in pairs. Dance: choosing and practising two working actions in pairs. Cool-down: shaking and relaxing.	● show strength in their actions ● make clear and recognisable working actions ● use their whole bodies

UNIT: Sailors

Enquiry questions	Learning objectives	Teaching activities	Learning outcomes
Can we practise working actions in groups?	● Practise different pathways and formations while marching, stopping and saluting. ● Practise marching in lines in formation. ● In pairs and then in groups, practise the hornpipe, thinking of formation. ● Try out and practise rhythmic movement phrases for pulling in the sheets (sails). ● Develop and refine own choice of working action. ● Vary level and positioning (relationship) within the groups.	Warm-up: practising marching step with a zigzag pathway; practising marching step in lines in formation; practising standing to attention to salute. Development: practising and refining hornpipe actions in pairs; practising different ways of pulling in the sheets using different directions. Dance: trying out two working actions in groups of four; practising and refining rhythmic phrases. Cool-down: walking into a space, swaying and circling.	● work well in groups ● have tried different formations or levels ● collaborate and work together to create and refine their working actions
Can we perform a sailors' dance?	● Practise and refine hornpipe in groups. ● Practise and refine group working actions. ● Create and perform a class dance.	Warm-up: jogging in time to the music; practising hornpipe steps in groups. Development: practising and refining two group working actions; combining different actions to create a six-part class dance. Dance: practise and refine class dance. Cool-down: walking slowly into a space, stretching and flopping.	● combine and remember the sequence of actions.

Cross-curricular links

History: a history topic about journeys might be the starting point for this series of lessons. By researching and discussing life on board ship at the time of the *Cutty Sark*, children will have found out something about the types of jobs that sailors were expected to do.
Music: singing sea shanties; listening and responding to hornpipe music.
Science: learning about forces, anchors and winches.
PSHE: working collaboratively in pairs or groups.
ICT: visiting the *Cutty Sark* website.

Resources

A cassette or CD player; 'Portsmouth' by Mike Oldfield (from *Music Wonderland* or *The Best of Elements*) or other hornpipe music; tambour; bells; photocopiable page 126.

Display

A variety of pictures of tall ships and tea clippers, such as the *Cutty Sark*.

 What work did sailors do on the tall ships?

What you need and preparation

You will need: a CD or tape player; 'Portsmouth' by Mike Oldfield; a tambour.

In the classroom, talk about the tea clippers with the children. If time permits, sing some sea shanties together.

Discuss also the particular arrangements for changing and going to the hall for PE.

What to do

Warm-up
8 mins

Ensure the children are well spaced to start the warm-up.

Start by asking the children to tap one foot in time to the music, then encourage them to make a pattern of taps (left, left, left or right, right, right; front/back, front/back).

Encourage them to step out, walking around the hall in time with the music (or light taps on the tambour). Prompt them to swing their arms and make good use of the space.

Encourage the children to practise using all directions and different pathways (figure of eight, zigzag and so on). Use the signal *Change* to prompt them to change direction.

Ask the children to try some other steps to this accompaniment and to make up a step pattern to the hornpipe music by linking two travelling actions together.

Encourage exploration and practise of ideas. For example, walk, walk, walk, walk, jump, jump or tap, tap, tap, tap, side-step, side-step, side-step. Suggest that they try some actions on the spot and some travelling.

Ask the children if they have seen a hornpipe, and if so to show or describe it to you. Listen to part of the music together then ask the children to try to make up a step pattern to the hornpipe music by linking two travelling actions.

Development
14 mins

Select one of the children's ideas for the whole class to try, or teach this step: Step forward onto the right foot and hop on the right foot. Step forward onto the left foot and hop on the left foot. Repeat.

Ask the children individually to practise the phrase, developing a step-hop sequence.

Then ask them to practise the same steps moving diagonally to the right, and diagonally to the left.

Now help them to add an arm action. They could choose their own or you could teach them one of the following:
● Right arm folded in front of the body, left arm folded behind, changing as the steps change (see Diagram 1).
● Right hand to forehead in a searching pose on right step forward and left hand to forehead in a searching pose on left foot forward (see Diagram 2).

Diagram 1

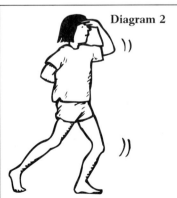
Diagram 2

Learning objectives
● Listen, travel and create step patterns to the music of the hornpipe.
● Learn a basic hornpipe step and create one.
● Practise some simple working action phrases.
● Begin to use different levels and directions in working actions.
● Create a simple pattern of dance phrases in twos.

Lesson organisation
Discussion and songs in the classroom; individual warm-up and development; paired dance; individual cool-down; teacher-led classroom review.

Vocabulary
hornpipe
on the lookout
climbing the rigging
exaggerate

Sailors

Encourage everyone to link their chosen travelling action and a hornpipe step, for example individual travelling action and step-hop sequence. Encourage regular rhythm and give guidelines of when to change from the travelling action to the hornpipe step.

Remind the children of the discussion in the classroom about the different jobs that are done on board a ship. Encourage their suggestions for jobs they could mime and then try the following:

● Rowing. Ask the children to sit down in a space and try a rowing action. Encouraging them to reach forward with both hands and then pull back strongly. Develop the rhythm of the action using words – *Reach and pull, reach and pull* or percussion, and emphasise a strong pull then relax and reach. Practise this and then ask the children to try it in other positions, such as kneeling or standing. Help them to exaggerate the action, making it larger than life, using the whole body.

● On the look out. Ask the children to think about what being 'on the look out' means on board ship. Ask them to try out ways of performing these actions to the music. Encourage them to stretch and look. Together, go on to develop it into a phrase of actions, for example walk, walk, walk and stop, pull out long telescope and look first of all in one direction, turn around and then look in another direction or climb and look, climb and look.

Using the children's ideas where possible, practise with the class a number of possibilities, using different directions and levels, such as high and forward, out to each side; low to the left and so on. Then ask the children to choose three places to look for incorporation into a sequence. Encourage large, exaggerated actions and develop them into a phrase, using different levels and different directions.

 Dance
In pairs, ask the children to choose one of these working actions to practise in time with a partner. Encourage them to think about their positioning (for example one behind the other, moving alternately) and to practise and repeat the rhythm of the action. They could also then try to make up a working action of their own.

 Cool-down
Ask the children to space out and walk lightly around the room, swinging their arms strongly and then gently.

Standing with their feet slightly apart, ask them to step to the left and reach and look and hold the stretch, step to the right and reach and look and hold the stretch. Tell the children to repeat this sequence.

Classroom review
Ask the class to think of other types of work that sailors would have had to do on board ship.

Assessing learning outcomes
How well are the children responding to and moving in time with the music? Are they contributing and developing their own ideas for the hornpipe and working actions?

35 mins Can we practise the hornpipe?

What you need and preparation

You will need: a CD or tape player; 'Portsmouth' by Mike Oldfield; a tambour.

In the classroom, remind the children of the key qualities of each working action. Continue the discussion from last week about tall ships, sailors' jobs on board and the sailors' hornpipe.

Remind the children of the arrangements for changing, getting to the hall and doing PE.

What to do

8 mins Warm-up

In a space, ask the children to bounce lightly on the spot. Then ask them to practise the side-step to the tap of a tambour making good use of the space. Encourage them to change direction (for example, eight steps in each direction). Encourage light footwork.

Teach another hornpipe action: heel tap to front with alternate heels.

Then encourage the children to tap the right heel to front right and the left heel to front left, with arms folded in front of the body at shoulder height (see Diagram 3). Emphasise a rhythmic action, keeping in time with the music. Then encourage the children to try a different hornpipe step.

Diagram 3

14 mins Development

In pairs, ask the children to choose, practise and clarify their own hornpipe step and then to show it to a partner. Tell them to try each other's and then to combine the steps into a sequence.

Now tell them to practise the hornpipe steps with their partners. Encourage the pairs to keep in time with the music and each other. Help them to decide on their starting position (side by side, facing each other or one behind the other) and to clarify their step actions.

Ask the children to practise their pair sequence, adding their own travelling actions towards each other. Remind them to start away from their partner. Encourage them to think of other

Diagram 4

ways that they can make their hornpipe special, for example using different directions in their relationship to each other (away from and towards each other, sideways, apart and together, forward and back).

Ask them to remember some of the other working actions that might have been performed by the sailors and to suggest some ideas of their own. Encourage them to try the following:

● Climbing the rigging. Ask the children to reach up high with one hand and the opposite foot to try out a climbing action to the rhythm of the music (see Diagram 4). Practise, and encourage a phrase that is repeated (for example climb and climb and climb and pause). When they have practised this with the music, advise them to stretch and look on the pause (to look out to sea or to look at the sails).

Learning objectives
● Practise side-step to the hornpipe.
● Refine other hornpipe ideas.
● Practise other working action phrases.
● Create and practise a pattern of dance phrases in twos.

Lesson organisation
Classroom discussion; individual warm-up; paired and individual development; paired dance; individual cool-down; teacher-led classroom review in pairs.

Vocabulary
scrubbing the decks
climbing the rigging
rhythm

Sailors

● Scrubbing the decks. Ask the children to show you a scrubbing action to the music. Encourage strong pushing and pulling actions, first of all with one hand and then with the other. Advise them to make the actions as large as possible, but to maintain the rhythm of the action. Try forwards and backwards and side to side. Develop a rhythmic phrase, for example scrub and scrub and scrub and scrub and ring out the cloth (or dip the brush in water). Ask them to try another position (standing or kneeling) and to try out other variations using a mop or a brush. Help them to develop a rhythmic phrase.

 Dance

Working with a partner, ask the children to choose one of these working actions to practise in time with a partner. Can they also practise one of their own or one from last week?

Ask the children to combine the hornpipe (travel and step) with one working action, and to practise linking these movements in pairs.

Cool-down

Ask the children to skip around lightly on their own, then skip on the spot, gradually slowing to a halt. Then ask them to stretch and look, stretch and look in two different directions.

Classroom review
Ask the children to discuss and plan their hornpipe movements with their partner.

Assessing learning outcomes
Are the children able to refine their movements for the hornpipe? Are they developing the working actions into rhythmic phrases?

(35 mins) What other jobs do sailors do on board ship?

What you need and preparation

You will need: a CD or cassette player; 'Portsmouth' by Mike Oldfield; a tambour.

In the classroom, recap the hornpipe sequence the children planned last week and the working actions on board ship.

What to do

(7 mins) Warm-up

Ask the children to practise walking in curving pathways in time with 'Portsmouth'. Then practise slip change of step to this music. In pairs, ask them to practise hornpipe steps.

(15 mins) Development

Ask the children about other jobs that sailors do on board ship. Then ask them to try out their ideas for the following actions:

● Sewing the nets. Encourage the children to enlarge and exaggerate their ideas to develop a motif or phrase that can be repeated. For example, needle down and up, down and up… reach to the side and pull the net along (towards the centre of the body). Repeat and practise, clarifying the action (sew in and out and in and out and move the nets along).

● Hauling in the anchor. Ask the children to think about what anchors are used for and how heavy they might be. Ask them to imagine pulling on a rope to haul the anchor in. Develop a phrase of action – pull and pull and pull and rest, pull and pull and pull and rest. Encourage them to clarify then exaggerate the action. Tell them to repeat the phrase a few times, then think about doing this in another position (kneeling or on the other side of the body).

● Turning the winch. Ask the children if they know what a winch is. Ask them to imagine that the winch is huge and that they are to turn it around. Let the children practise strong ciruclar movements horizontally in front of them (like polishing a table – see Diagram 5). Then encourage them to circle forwards and backwards vertically (like a wheel). Then help them to circle to wind the winch from side to side (over their heads and down to the floor).

Invite them to choose one of these ways to practise with a partner, and to try to do it in time with each other, matching each other's actions.

(10 mins) Dance

Ask the pairs to choose one of these working actions to practise together. Encourage them to decide on their position in relation to each other (one behind the other, matching and so on).

(3 mins) Cool-down

Ask the children to walk around until they are in a space and then to shake and relax, shake and relax.

Classroom review

Ask the children: *Which of the working actions did you like best? What were the special qualities that were needed?*

Assessing learning outcomes

Can the children show strength in their actions? Are the working actions clear and recognisable? Are they using their whole bodies?

Learning objectives
● Practise pathways and changing direction while walking to a beat.
● Revise and practise a hornpipe sequence.
● Practise other working action phrases.
● Create and practise a pattern of dance phrases in twos.

Lesson organisation
Classroom revision; warm-up and development individually and in pairs; individual cool-down; teacher-led classroom review.

Vocabulary
hauling in the anchor
turning the winch
sewing the nets
motif
phrase

Diagram 5

35 mins Can we practise working actions in groups?

Learning objectives
● Practise different pathways while marching, stopping and saluting.
● Practise marching in lines in formation.
● In pairs and then in groups, practise the hornpipe, thinking of formation.
● Try out and practise rhythmic movement phrases for pulling in the sheets.
● Develop and refine own choice of working action.
● Vary level and positioning (relationship) within groups.

Lesson organisation
Classroom discussion; individual and paired warm-up; paired development; dance in groups; individual cool-down; teacher-led classroom review.

Vocabulary
pulling in the sheets
sails
salute
halt
formation
stand to attention

What you need and preparation

You will need: a CD or tape player; 'Portsmouth' by Mike Oldfield; a tambour; a bell.

Before going to the hall, discuss with the children ways of practising and refining working actions on board ship and explain what is meant by 'pulling in the sheets'.

Also discuss with them the special arrangements for changing with reminders about getting to the hall and doing PE.

What to do

5 mins Warm-up
Ensure everyone is well spaced to start the warm-up.

Ask the children to practise a light, happy, walking step individually, using curving pathways. Look for good spacing.

Encourage them to practise a firm, marching step in straight lines with a zigzag pathway, individually then in pairs, following or side by side.

Ask them all to practise standing to attention to salute (give guidance to prepare to stop, for example, say *Ready, and halt*).

Then tell them to stretch and reach, stretch and look.

13 mins Development
In the same pairs as in the last lesson, if possible, ask the children to practise their hornpipe actions. Remind them of the two parts – a travelling action and a hornpipe step – and give them time to practise and refine their actions in time with the music. Help them to clarify their positions in relation to each other (side by side or facing each other or one following the other). Each pair could join another to practise these actions, thinking of their group formation.

Then ask the children to try out the following action:
● Pulling in the sheets. Ask the pairs to try out some of the actions that sailors might have done to pull in the sails. Encourage them to try out their ideas and then emphasise a strong pull and relax, pull and relax rhythm. Practise this and then encourage the children to think of other ways of pulling in the sails. Look for variations in the children's responses and try some of their ideas as a class (for example with short sharp tugs or with long continuous pulling actions; with two hands or one hand). Encourage everyone to try pulling from different directions (from above or the side) and practise these, developing rhythmic movement phrases to the accompaniment.

14 mins Dance
Ask each pair to join another pair and, in their groups of four, to decide which two working actions they want to try out as a group. Encourage them to practise one of these, developing and refining their rhythmic movement phrases.

Advise them to experiment with different positions or group formations and see if they can use different levels.

In this way, ask them to discuss and then practise their other chosen working action.

3 mins Cool-down
Individually, ask the children to walk around the hall and then stop in a space to practise swaying and circling.

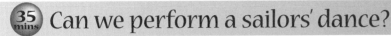

Classroom review

Ask the children to discuss in their groups how they might develop or improve their ideas for next week. Check that most variations are represented.

Assessing learning outcomes

How well do the children work in groups? Have they tried different formations or levels? Are they able to collaborate and work together to create and refine their working actions?

35 mins Can we perform a sailors' dance?

What you need and preparation

You will need: a CD or cassette player; 'Portsmouth' by Mike Oldfield; a tambour; bell.
   Ask the children to discuss their plans for the group dances.

What to do

5 mins Warm-up

Ask everyone to jog in time to the music. Emphasise high knees in a light, bouncy step.
   Then ask the children to practise and refine their hornpipe steps and then their hornpipe actions in groups. Encourage different formations and starting positions (for example towards, away from, side by side, back to back, following in a line, in a circle).

18 mins Development

In their groups, ask the children to practise and refine group working actions from the last few weeks. Gradually encourage them to combine the different actions to create a class dance. This could be done in six parts:
● Some groups jogging, some groups performing a step pattern towards the ship.
● Captain's coming (bell ringing) – gather in lines and stand to attention and salute.
● March in lines (two or four lines – could be two lines going one way and two the other way in formation) and stand to attention and salute.
● Off to work – each group selects one of the working actions to perform to the music.
● Captain's coming (bell ringing) – march into lines and stand to attention and salute, then each group practises their other chosen working action.
● Follow my leader – hornpipe actions in groups then their choice of group formation to finish.

10 mins Dance

Help the whole class to practise and perform the six-part dance as detailed in the Development section.

2 mins Cool-down

Ask the children to find a space and walk slowly to stretch and flop, stretch and flop.

Classroom review

Ask the groups what they did to improve their group actions and how they think they could improve parts of the dance (timing, clarification of actions, formations and so on).

Assessing learning outcomes

How well could the children combine and remember the sequence of actions? Can they review and evaluate their own and others' performances?

PRIMARY FOUNDATIONS: Physical education Ages 7–9

Learning objectives
● Practise and refine hornpipe actions in groups.
● Practise and refine group working actions.
● Create and perform a class dance.

Lesson organisation
Classroom discussion; individual and group warm-up; development in groups then as a whole-class; whole-class dance; individual cool-down; teacher-led classroom review.

Vocabulary
climbing the rigging
pulling in the sheets
turning the winch
hauling in the anchor
sewing the nets

Dinosaurs and All That Rubbish

This series of lessons uses the story *Dinosaurs and All That Rubbish* by Michael Foreman (Puffin Books) as a stimulus for dance. Using the sequence of the story and the environmental theme, it explores contrasting movement qualities and enables children, within a clear framework, to use movement imaginatively and expressively. It also gradually introduces some elements of a simple circle country dance as a celebratory conclusion to the story.

It is essential that the story is read with the children in the classroom before the dance sessions begin. This could be part of the Literacy Hour or in its own right. Children can be encouraged to select some of the key elements of the story to sequence, and to discuss some of the key environmental issues, such as pollution. Asking the children what they already know about dinosaurs will be a good starting point for exploring, selecting and refining the qualities of their movements.

This unit requires an indoor hall space. It consists of six sessions, allowing 30–40 minutes of activity per session. The children will create, perform, think about and appreciate dances individually, in pairs, in groups or as a whole class.

UNIT: Dinosaurs and All That Rubbish

Enquiry questions	Learning objectives	Teaching activities	Learning outcomes
How do you build a rocket to go to the Moon?	● Practise moving different parts of the body and travelling in time to the beat, individually then following a partner. ● Explore differences between happy and unhappy body movements and posture. ● Explore and practise working actions within the context of the story. ● Develop rhythmic phrases of movement individually and in pairs and begin to link these together.	Warm-up: sitting, listening and clapping in time with the beat; developing a phrase of claps and taps; moving to the beat; walking in time with the beat; practising sequence with a partner. Development: practising still shapes to show unhappiness and happiness; walking with heavy steps; building a rocket; making and refining a phrase of movements. Dance: practising working action individually and with a partner. Cool-down: skipping around the space; stretching and relaxing.	Children: ● exaggerate and use their whole bodies in the movements ● create a rhythm for and clarify the working actions
Can we search on a star?	● Practise different ways of moving parts of the body and stepping in time to the beat. ● Practise light steps. ● Use different levels and directions to search on a star. ● Link a phrase of actions – stepping and searching.	Warm-up: tapping feet to the beat; moving to the beat and developing into a phrase; walking then skipping; linking movements and practising with a partner. Development: practising light, 'weightless' steps; jumping, leaping and turning in slow motion; searching on a star; reaching in different directions; linking actions into a phrase. Dance: practising the sequence to build a rocket; making on-board rocket actions; practising searching on a star. Cool-down: marching on the spot, gradually slowing.	● change from strong working actions to light weightlessness
How do dinosaurs move?	● Explore different ways of greeting a partner and link them with travelling steps. ● Explore and think about different types of dinosaur – their shapes and how they might move. ● Link selected movement ideas into short phrases of action.	Warm-up: tapping feet to the beat; moving body parts; travelling; greeting a partner without touching; linking actions together. Development: practising dinosaur shapes; practising dinosaur movements; making a phrase of dinosaur movements and shapes. Dance: selecting and linking phrases; practising and refining sequences. Cool-down: side-stepping, slowing to a sideways walk; looking and reaching; relaxing.	● use their imagination to explore different types (shapes and sizes) of dinosaur ● begin to try some original ideas
How did the dancing dinosaurs break up the roads?	● Practise selected ways of greeting a partner and link them with travelling steps. ● Practise different types of dinosaur actions and dance steps. ● Explore pushing actions with different parts of the body in different directions. ● Explore different ways of waking and stretching. ● Link selected phrases of movement into short sequences of action.	Warm-up: shrugging shoulders in time with the beat; moving bodies and travelling to the beat; greeting a partner; linking actions together. Development: practising dinosaur shapes and movements; linking three yawning phrases; practising dinosaur dance. Dance: linking dinosaur phrases; dancing as dinosaurs. Cool-down: breathing in slowly, raising the arms; stretching and relaxing.	● remember their phrases of action and link them together ● refine their actions

UNIT 2: Dinosaurs and All That Rubbish

Enquiry questions	Learning objectives	Teaching activities	Learning outcomes
Can we perform a happy dance?	● Practise different types of dinosaur actions and dance steps. ● Explore and develop working actions – different ways of cleaning up the rubbish. ● Create a happy dance to celebrate in pairs and as a group. ● Link selected movement ideas into short phrases of actions.	Warm-up: twisting hips and bouncing on the spot to the beat; greeting a partner, clarifying the action; linking actions together. Development: practising dinosaur actions; practising cleaning up the rubbish. Dance: learning a version of the 'Circassian circle'. Cool-down: stretching and holding their breath; breathing in slowly and out quickly.	● distinguish light and happy, strong and slow qualities in their actions ● follow instructions and perform dances
How can we tell the story in dance?	● Practise and improve the 'Circassian circle' dance. ● Practise, perform and link phrases of actions to tell the story of *Dinosaurs and All That Rubbish*. ● Appreciate the work of themselves and others and consider ways in which they might refine their performances.	Warm-up: moving elbows in time with the beat; tapping feet; linking actions together. Development: practising working actions, searching on a star, dinosaur phrases and 'Circassian circle'. Dance: performing a complete dance. Cool-down: stretching; breathing in quickly and out slowly.	● perform a dance ● think about and describe what they had done and think of ways in which they could make it better.

Cross-curricular links
Literacy: writing about environmental issues.
Geography: investigating the problems of pollution.

Resources
Copies of *Dinosaurs and All That Rubbish* by Michael Foreman; a CD or tape player; 'Hulichan Roundabout'; *The Snowman* theme, 'Floating in the air'; 'The Elephant' from *Carnival of the Animals* by Saint-Saëns; music for a 'Circassian circle' – 'Lord of the Dance'; tambour; tambourine; wood blocks; small bells; cymbals.

Display
Pictures and models of dinosaurs.

⏱35 mins How do you build a rocket to go to the Moon?

What you need and preparation

You will need a CD or tape player; some country dance music such as 'Hulichan Roundabout' or similar country dance rhythm; percussion such as a tambour.

Read through the text of *Dinosaurs and All That Rubbish* in the classroom, discussing the key elements of the story and the environmental issues contained within it; encourage a good discussion about the man in the story being unhappy about living on Earth.

What to do

⏱6 mins Warm-up

Ask the children to sit and listen to the rhythm of the music and then clap in time with the beat. See if they can clap for eight beats and listen for eight beats, and then for four and two.

Ask them to think of and try some different ways they could keep in time to the same beat (for example clicking fingers, tapping knees or the floor or swaying). Encourage them to try several ways and then choose two, developing them into a phrase (for example four claps and four taps).

Encourage them to feel the beat in their bodies by moving part of their bodies to the beat (nodding head, shrugging shoulders, knees knocking, tapping feet and so on). Encourage larger movements while keeping in time to the beat. Ask them to develop a phrase (such as four shrugs and four taps) and to think about and choose the position they could be in (standing, sitting or kneeling).

Ask them to try walking around the hall in time with the beat. Encourage them to use all the space and to use their arms as they go. Count the beat for them and ask them to turn to move in another direction after eight steps (count to seven and say *Turn*). Some children will find this easier than others. Encourage those who can keep in time with the beat to be more precise with their actions, and encourage others to relax, listen and count as they move. Help by saying, *Ready, and, turn* rather than *Six, seven, eight*.

Ask the children to make up or try some other steps to the beat (for example side-stepping or skipping). Encourage them to keep moving until their pulse is raised by trying several ways. Help them to change their action every sixteen or eight beats.

Ask them to choose two steps to make into a sequence (for example eight walks, eight skips; eight in one direction, eight in another) in time with the beat.

In pairs, ask them to describe and then show their partner their two steps. As soon as possible, encourage the partner to follow the sequence of steps. Practise and then change over leaders. Encourage light, happy steps.

⏱15 mins Development

Remind the children of the discussion in the classroom about the man being unhappy about living on Earth. Ask them to show you one, then other, still shapes which demonstrate unhappiness or happiness. Can they tell the difference? Ask them if they can repeat the stepping sequence they have just tried, imagining that they were very unhappy. Ask them to describe and show the differences. Encourage them to practise the sequence using some of their ideas (with heavy steps or with a stooping body posture). Help them to exaggerate these.

Ask them if they can remember what the man thought, what he decided to do and how he did it. (He thought the moon looked good and so decided to build a rocket to go to the moon by

Learning objectives
● Practise moving different parts of the body and travelling in time to a beat, individually then following a partner.
● Explore differences between happy and unhappy body movements and posture.
● Explore and practise working actions within the context of the story.
● Develop rhythmic phrases of movement individually and in pairs and begin to link these together.

Lesson organisation
Classroom introduction; individual and paired warm-up and development; paired dance; individual cool-down; teacher-led classroom review.

Vocabulary
shrugging
nodding
clicking
tapping
happy
unhappy
cutting
dragging
chopping
swinging
pushing
pulling

cutting down trees and digging for coal.) Ask the children to try different ways the workers might cut down trees (such as sawing and chopping). Use a strong, regular rhythm as the accompaniment for the working actions. Starting from the mimed action, help them to exaggerate the moves and to feel the rhythm of the action. Select some children to demonstrate examples of the rhythm (for example saw, saw, saw and rest).

Choose one of the children's ideas or encourage them all to try chopping actions with an imaginary large axe (swing over the shoulder and chop then relax, swing over the shoulder and chop then relax). Help them to feel the strength of the chopping action. Ask them to practise a phrase of three actions several times (chop and lift, chop and lift, chop and lift).

Ask them all to try a phrase of pulling and pushing backwards and forwards with a saw (pull and push, pull and push). With a partner, ask them to decide how they could do this together to feel the action and reaction of the movement. Repeat, asking the children how they might clarify the action. Ask them to show how they might hold the saw and choose different positions they might use (standing, kneeling) and draw attention to the strong parts of the action.

Ask the children what sort of tools might they use to dig out the coal (a pickaxe, spade, machine and so on) and to show you how they might do that. Encourage them to repeat the action several times to feel the rhythm and then make them into a phrase of movements (dig, lift and throw; dig, lift and throw; dig, lift and throw). Help them to vary the action (for example using the other hand, other side, a different position) and to think how they could refine it.

Ask them what working actions they might have to do to build a rocket to reach the stars. *Can you remember any of the pictures in the book?* Encourage them to try hammering (bang, bang, bang in one place; bang, bang, bang in another place).

Encourage them to think about lifting, pushing or pulling heavy loads (for example, push and push and push and rest). In each of these actions, encourage movements to be larger than life, with rhythmic phrases for the action and recovery. Ask them what they must remember when they are lifting heavy things. (Bending their knees, not their backs.)

 Dance

Ask the children to choose one of the working actions to practise individually. Ask them to find a partner and to show each other their working action. Choosing one action at a time, ask them to decide how they are going to practise it together. Are they going to work at the same time or alternately? What levels will they use? What could be the starting position?

Ask them to practise both working actions, thinking how they might change from one to another. Ask them to repeat the actions several times, encouraging them to think how they could make them clearer and larger.

 Cool-down

Ask the children to skip in and out around the hall, listening to the beat of the tambour (*da di da di da di*). Encourage them to gradually slow down until they are doing slow-motion steps. In a space, tell them to reach out to one side, to the other side, stretch up towards the ceiling and crouch down to the floor. Ask them to repeat this then lie down and relax.

Classroom review

Ask the children about the story. What did they think of the man using up all the resources and making such a mess on Earth?

Assessing learning outcomes

Are the children able to exaggerate and use their whole bodies in the movements? Are they able to create a rhythm for and clarify the working actions?

**Dinosaurs and
All That Rubbish**

(35 mins) Can we search on a star?

What you need and preparation
You will need: wood blocks; tambourine; small bells; music: 'Hulichan Roundabout';
The Snowman theme, 'Walking in the Air'.

In the classroom, remind the children of the story *Dinosaurs and All That Rubbish*.

What to do

(6 mins) Warm-up
Ask the children to stand in a space to listen to the rhythm of the music
('Hulichan Roundabout') and to tap one foot in time with the beat. See if they can
tap for eight beats with one foot and then for eight beats with the other foot, and
then try four and four, and two and two.

Ask them to remember and try some different ways they could keep in time to
the same beat (perhaps clicking fingers, touching elbows or swaying). Advise them
to try several ways and then choose two, developing a phrase (for example four
clicks and four hip sways). Encourage them to really feel the beat in their bodies and
encourage larger movements. Ask them to develop a phrase (such as four shrugs
and four taps) and to choose a different position they could be in (standing, sitting or kneeling).
Ask them if they can combine two ways (for example head nodding and foot tapping; swaying
and clapping).

Ask them to try walking (then skipping) around the hall in time with the beat. Then see if
they can remember and try some of the other ways they tried in the last lesson. Encourage
them to use all of the space and all of their bodies. Tell them to count the beat and to turn to
move in another direction after eight steps (count to seven and say *Turn*). Help them to change
their action every eight beats.

Ask them to practise two steps and link them together (for example eight side-steps, eight
skips) in time with the beat.

Organise the children into different pairings from last week and ask them to number
themselves 1 and 2. Number 1 describes and then shows their partner their two steps.
Encourage 2s to join in as soon as possible, following the sequence of steps. Tell everyone to
practise this a few times and then change over leaders.

Ask the pairs to decide on and then practise one way of travelling with their partner (side by
side or one behind the other).

(10 mins) Development
Ask the children to practise light, 'weightless' steps as if they were
astronauts on the Moon. Use a light bell sound to encourage light, slow steps.
Encourage them to move to the side as well as forwards and backwards.

Ask them to try and practise other weightless actions in turn:
● jumping
● leaping
● turning.

Help them to feel the light, suspended, slow-motion quality of each action.
Some very light music, such as *The Snowman* theme, could be used to
accompany this.

Ask the children to show you how they might search on a star, and how
they might look in all directions. Encourage them to develop these searching

actions into a phrase – step, step and turn and look one way; step, step and turn and look the other way or in another place. Ask them to link their actions into a phrase – step and search at one level, step and search at another level, using 'weightless' steps.

Diagram 6

Encourage them to practise reaching – looking as far as they can in one direction and then as far as they can in the other direction. Ask them to vary the level of the action, reaching up high and crouching down low (see Diagram 6) and to practise a phrase of these actions.

Tell them to think about which level they could start with (high, medium or low) and to choose a starting position at one.

Encourage them to move in different directions to search on a star by trying 'weightless' steps in each direction in turn. Help them to link together a phrase of actions – step and step and step and search at one level; step and step and step and search at another level.

 Dance

16 mins In pairs, ask the children to practise their sequence of working actions to build the rocket that they planned and tried last week.

Back on their own, ask the children to decide how they might sit or lie for the rocket's lift off. Ask them to check all the controls by pushing lots of buttons with short sharp movements to the accompaniment of taps on the wood block. Encourage them to use all the space in front of them (out to the side, above their head, down by their feet) and then to hold a position very still for the countdown.

Then tell them to imagine that they are on the flight and that they are weightless and trying to move about the rocket. Encourage them to try turning over, walking or reaching up for things to the sound of the bells.

Ask them to imagine that the rocket is landing on the Moon and to decide whether it is a bumpy or smooth landing. Ask them to practise some of the actions to your accompaniment of shaking and banging a tambourine.

Remind them of their sequence for searching on a star, using 'weightless' steps, looking in each direction in turn. Let them practise their phrase of actions – step and step and step and search at one level; step and step and step and search at another level.

3 mins **Cool-down**

Ask the children to march on the spot and then around the space, gradually changing to slower, lighter steps as you lighten the tap on the tambourine and slow the speed of the action.

Classroom review

Ask the children how they managed to represent the feeling of weightlessness. *Did you find this difficult? Why?*

Assessing learning outcomes

Are the children able to change from strong working actions to light 'weightlessness'?

(35 mins) How do dinosaurs move?

What you need and preparation

You will need: a CD or tape player; 'The Elephant' from *Carnival of the Animals* by Saint-Saëns; 'Hulichan Roundabout'; a tambourine; tambour; cymbals. A display of various pictures and models of dinosaurs in the classroom would be useful.

Talk about dinosaurs with the children. Ask them:
● What are they?
● What do they look like?
● How do they move? ·

What to do

(8 mins) Warm-up

Ask the children to tap one foot then the other foot in time with the beat of 'Hulichan Roundabout'. Encourage them to practise tapping for eight beats with one foot and then for eight beats with the other foot, and then try four and four, and two and two.

Ask them to practise some of the different ways they could keep in time to the same beat – moving part of their bodies and then moving around the hall. Ask them to choose and practise some of the ways of travelling they tried last week. Encourage them to use all of the space and use all of their bodies. Help them to change their action every eight or four beats.

In pairs, ask them to try out ways of greeting their partner without touching them (waving, winking, nodding, bowing, bobbing, jumping and so on – see Diagram 7). Help them to decide on two of these actions and then practise them together for a count of eight. Encourage them to think of different ways they can do this (for example alternately, at the same time, one greets for four beats then the other for four beats) and then to practise this together. So they would, for example, nod alternately for eight beats and four bobs together.

Ask them to link together some of these actions, for example keeping time, travel, greet, travel. Starting away from their partner in a space ask them to do the following:
● Keep in time with the beat for eight beats on the spot.
● Travel towards their partner using their favourite step for eight beats.
● Greet their partner for eight beats, using one of their ways.
● Travel with their partner for eight beats.
Encourage them to practise all of these actions several times.

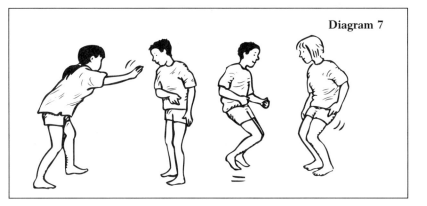

Diagram 7

(12 mins) Development

Ask the children to think about the different types of dinosaur that they discussed in the classroom, and the sort of shapes they might be (tall and wide, big and spiky, tall and thin or small and round). Ask them individually to step or skip slowly to the music ('The Elephant' from *Carnival of the Animals*) and when it stops to make one of the shapes (a variation of musical statues). Encourage them to think about spiky horns and jagged, sharp claws.

Move on to ask them to think how the dinosaurs might move. Encourage everyone to try out and practise some of the children's suggestions in turn, emphasising the quality of the movement rather than 'being' dinosaurs. They could try some or all of the following:

● slow, plodding steps (encourage steps in different directions – use the tambour as the accompaniment)
● heavy, stamping steps (use the tambour)
● quick, scampering steps (use the tambourine)
● large, swooping, soaring, circling flying movements (use light taps of the cymbal and a continuous sound).

Together, build up a phrase for each of these – step and step and step and stop or step, step, step; step, step, step, step, step, step, stop for quicker actions. Use tambourine taps as the accompaniment.

Encourage the children to think about the dinosaurs waking and stretching. Start with a big yawning action and develop it into a phrase – stre-e-e-etch and reach in one direction, curl, turn and stre-e-etch and reach in another direction.

Tell them to imagine the dinosaurs pushing and pressing the earth away. Then ask them to think about the different parts of their body that they could use to press and push the earth away (perhaps hands, backs, feet, bottoms and sides) and to try out the strong, slow actions. Help them to build this into a phrase using chosen parts of the body in turn – push and push and push and relax, and repeat this three times.

Encourage them to develop their ideas, pushing in different directions in turn (above their heads, to the side and forwards).

10 mins Dance

Ask the children to select and link three different pushing phrases.

Then ask them to practise and link together the phrases practised today:
● waking and stretching
● pushing in different directions with different parts of the body
● selected types of dinosaur action, each practised in turn.

Tell them to select a working action sequence and/or weightless actions to remember, practise and refine.

5 mins Cool-down

Ask the children to side-step around the hall in both directions, using all the space. Encourage them to keep the movement light and springy. Help them to slow down gradually to a sideways walk.

In a space, ask them to practise looking as far as they can in one direction and then as far as they can in the other direction. Advise them to vary the level of the action, reaching up high and crouching down low. Repeat this, then tell them to lie down to relax.

Classroom review
Ask the children to describe to a partner the shapes of the dinosaurs that they tried. Prompt their discussions by asking questions such as: *How did you move? What was special about your action?*

Assessing learning outcomes
Are the children able to use their imagination to explore different types (shapes and sizes) of dinosaur? Are they beginning to try some original ideas?

35 mins How did the dancing dinosaurs break up the roads?

Diagram 8

Learning objectives
● Practise selected ways of greeting a partner and link them with travelling steps.
● Practise different types of dinosaur actions and dance steps.
● Explore pushing actions with different parts of the body in different directions.
● Explore different ways of waking and stretching.
● Link selected phrases of movement into short sequences of action.

Lesson organisation
Classroom discussion; individual and paired warm-up; development and dance individually; individual cool-down; teacher-led classroom review in pairs.

What you need and preparation
You will need: a CD or tape player; copies of 'The Elephant' from *Carnival of the Animals* by Saint-Saëns and 'Hulichan Roundabout'; a tambourine; cymbals.

Before going to the hall, recap with the children what they know about dinosaurs and go through the section of *Dinosaurs and All That Rubbish* that concentrates on dinosaurs.

What to do

8 mins Warm-up
Ask the children to shrug their shoulders in time with the beat of 'Hulichan Roundabout'. Encourage them to practise this for eight beats and then try four and four, and two and two with alternate shoulders.

Ask them to remember and practise some of the other ways they could keep in time to the beat – moving part of their bodies and then moving around the hall. Ask them: *Can you remember some of the ways you tried last week?* Encourage them to use all of the space and all of their bodies. Help them to change their action every eight or four beats.

In pairs, ask them to discuss and then practise two ways of greeting their partner without touching them. Help them to exaggerate, clarify and refine their actions. This time, ask each pair to try and then practise two other ways of greeting their partner (for example shake hands, high fives, bottom touch – see Diagrams 8 and 9). Tell everyone to practise these three ways and then choose one to refine further.

Ask them to practise linking together some of these actions, for, example keeping time, travel, greet, travel. Starting away from their partner in a space, ask them to perform the following:
● keep in time with the beat for eight beats on the spot
● travel towards their partner using their favourite step for eight beats
● greet their partner for eight beats using one of their ways
● travel with their partner for eight beats.
Encourage them to practise these several times.

Vocabulary
shrug
alternate
plodding
stamping
scampering
swooping
soaring
waking
stretching
yawning

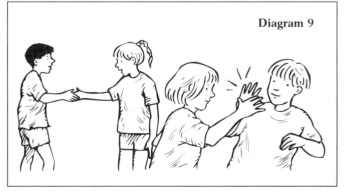

Diagram 9

 Development

Ask the children to think about the different types of dinosaur that they tried to make last week (tall and wide, big and spiky, tall and thin, small and round). Ask them individually to step or skip to the music and when it stops to make one of the shapes. Remind them to think about spiky horns and jagged, sharp claws.

Ask them if they can remember and show you how some of the dinosaurs moved. Practise some of their ways together, again emphasising the quality of the movement rather than 'being' dinosaurs:

● slow, plodding steps (encourage steps in different directions – tambour accompaniment)
● heavy, stamping steps (tambour)
● quick, scampering steps (tambourine)
● large, swooping, soaring, circling flying movements (light taps of the cymbal and a continuous sound).

Encourage the children to practise each phrase in turn, helping them to distinguish the particular qualities of each action. Encourage them to listen and respond to the accompaniment.

Ask them to think about the dinosaurs waking up and stretching. Tell them to start with a big yawning action and develop that into a phrase: stre-e-etch, yawn and reach in one direction, curl, turn and stre-e-etch, yawn and reach in another direction. Practise linking three yawning phrases together. Use words as the accompaniment.

Encourage the children to think about the dinosaurs pushing and pressing the earth away. Encourage them to think about the different parts of their body that they could use (hands, backs, feet, sides and bottoms) and to try out the strong, slow actions. Build these into a phrase using chosen parts of the body in turn: push and push and push and relax (three times).

Go on to develop their ideas for pushing in different directions in turn (overhead, to the side, forwards).

Then ask the children to think how the dinosaurs might dance. Ask them to listen to 'The Elephant' from *Carnival of the Animals* and to try some of their ideas. Help them to develop a phrase of actions by practising steps, turns and jumps in turn, using either slow, ponderous or slow, strong qualities. Ask them to repeat this and to choose a starting position.

14 mins Dance

Ask the children to practise and link together the dinosaur phrases they have practised:
● waking and stretching (three times), yawning phrases
● pushing in different directions with different parts of the body (three times)
● selected type of dinosaur actions, each practised in turn
● dancing dinosaurs.

3 mins Cool-down

Ask the children to breathe in slowly, raising their arms above their heads. Encourage them to stretch then breathe out, letting the whole body go floppy. Do this together several times, with regular, even timing.

Classroom review

Ask the children to describe their dinosaur dance to a partner. Did their partner include stepping and turning?

Assessing learning outcomes

Are the children able to remember their phrases of action and link them together? Can they refine their actions?

Can we perform a happy dance?

What you need and preparation

You will need: a CD or tape player; 'Circassian circle' – 'Lord of the Dance'; 'Hulichan Roundabout'; 'The Elephant' from *Carnival of the Animals*; a tambour; tambourine; cymbals.

In the classroom, talk about the story with the children, particularly the section in which the dinosaurs clear the rubbish.

What to do

10 mins Warm-up

Ask the children to twist their hips in time with the beat. Practise twisting for eight beats, then clapping for eight beats. Alternate twisting hips and bouncing on the spot. Repeat several times, reminding the children to keep in time with the accompaniment ('Hulichan Roundabout').

Ask them to remember and then practise some of the steps they tried last week. Encourage them to use all the space and to change their action every eight beats.

In pairs, ask them to choose and practise two ways of greeting their partner and to think how they might make their action clearer or more expansive.

Ask them to think of and try different ways of turning their partner (such as linking elbows, with two hands, with one hand high – see Diagram 10) and to choose and practise two ways.

Diagram 10

Now ask them to practise linking together some of these actions, for example keeping time, travel, greet, turn. Starting away from their partner in a space, ask them to:
- keep in time with the beat for eight beats on the spot
- travel towards their partner using their favourite step for eight beats
- greet their partner for eight beats using one of their ways
- turn their partner for eight beats.

Encourage them to practise all of these several times, emphasising light, happy steps.

10 mins Development

Encourage the children to practise different types of dinosaur actions and dance steps:
- waking and stretching (three times), yawning phrases
- pushing in different directions with different parts of the body (three times)
- selected type of dinosaur action
- dancing dinosaurs (to 'The Elephant').

Learning objectives
- Practise different types of dinosaur actions and dance steps.
- Explore and develop working actions – different ways of cleaning up the rubbish.
- Create a happy dance to celebrate in pairs and as a group.
- Link selected movement ideas into short phrases of action.

Lesson organisation
Classroom discussion; individual and paired warm-up and practice; class dance; individual cool-down; teacher-led classroom review.

Vocabulary
twist
waking
stretching

**Dinosaurs and
All That Rubbish**

In pairs, encourage the children to take it in turns to watch their partners and then to help them to think of how they could refine the actions.

Ask them to think how the dinosaurs might have cleared up the mess. Using these slow heavy qualities, use some of the children's ideas or practise a sweeping action – swe-e-e-ep and pause and swe-e-e-ep and rest (to 'The Elephant' or a percussion accompaniment).

Now tell the children to practise another clearing up action with a partner (for example lifting rubbish into a bin). Help them to develop a rhythmic phrase and enlarge their actions.

Ask them to combine actions with their partners deciding how they might work together (for example, both doing the same action – lifting heavy loads; one sweeping, one scooping up rubbish).

12 mins Dance

Teach the class a version of the 'Circassian circle'. With everyone in a circle facing the middle, number the children alternately 1 and 2. Ask everyone to take three steps into the middle of the circle and three steps back again, bringing their feet together on each fourth beat. The children will find this easier to do if they hold hands.

Number 1s then take three steps into the middle and back, then the 2s do the same, except that they turn to face the number ones as they move back to their place. Practise this together.

Each number 1 and number 2 then join hands to turn each other one way for eight beats then the other way for eight beats. They then face anticlockwise, walking side by side around the circle for 16 beats, turning to the middle on the last two beats, ready to start and repeat again. Practise this several times to the tune 'Lord of the Dance'.

3 mins Cool-down

Ask the children to space out and breathe in slowly, raising their arms above their heads. Encourage them to stretch and hold their breath, then breathe out quickly letting the whole body suddenly go floppy. Do this several times then repeat with regular, even timing.

Classroom review
Ask the children to explain the difference between their happy dance and the strong, slow dinosaur dance.

Assessing learning outcomes
Can the children distinguish the light and happy; strong and slow qualities in their actions? How well do they follow instructions and perform the dances?

35 mins How can we tell the story in dance?

What you need and preparation

You will need: a CD or tape player; 'Circassian circle' – 'Lord of the Dance'; 'Hulichan Roundabout'; 'The Elephant' from *Carnival of the Animals* by Saint-Saëns; tambour; tambourine; cymbals.

What to do

7 mins Warm-up

Ask the children to move their elbows to touch each other and away from each other in time with the beat (*Hulichan Roundabout* or similar country dance). Practise this together for eight beats then try tapping one foot for eight beats. Then moving elbows for eight beats, and eight beats tapping the other foot.

Repeat several times, keeping in time with the accompaniment.

Ask the children to choose and practise one way of keeping in time. Then tell them to choose one of the steps they have practised previously.

In pairs, ask them to choose and practise one way of greeting their partners then one way of turning their partners.

Now see if they can practise linking together these actions:
● individually keep in time with the beat for eight beats on the spot
● travel towards their partner for eight beats
● greet their partner for eight beats using one of their ways
● try turning their partner for eight beats
● travel into a space for eight beats, ready to start again.

Encourage them to practise the sequence several times.

15 mins Development

Ask the children to practise the following dances that they have performed over the last few sessions. In turn:
● cutting down trees
● building a rocket
● searching on a star
● dinosaurs waking and stretching and yawning (see Diagram 11)

Diagram 11

● pushing in different directions with different parts of the body
● dancing dinosaurs
● cleaning up the rubbish.

Learning objectives
● Practise and improve the 'Circassian circle' dance.
● Practise, perform and link phrases of actions to tell the story of *Dinosaurs and All That Rubbish*.
● Appreciate the work of themselves and others and consider ways in which they might refine their performances.

Lesson organisation
Individual and paired warm-up; individual development; whole-class dance; individual cool-down; teacher-led classroom review.

Vocabulary
practice
refine
dinosaur

**Dinosaurs and
All That Rubbish**

Practise the 'Circassian circle'. If appropriate, add a clap after each three steps into the middle of the circle (one, two, three, clap; one, two, three, back). Help the children to discuss and think of ways they could refine their actions.

Dance

Ask all the children to perform the whole dance together at first. Then split the class into two, to watch each half in turn. Encourage the children to think about ways in which it might be improved (both when performing and observing), and then repeat as a whole-class performance.

Cool-down

Ask the children to find their own space and breathe in, quickly raising their arms above their heads. Encourage them to stretch and hold their breath then breathe out slowly, letting the whole body go floppy very slowly. Do this several times, then repeat for the final time with regular, even timing.

Classroom review

Ask the children what they enjoyed most about performing and watching the dance.

Assessing learning outcomes

How well did the children perform the dance? Are they able to think about and describe what they have done and think of ways in which they could make it better?

**Follow-up
activity**
Ask the children to create their own dance in fours and video a performance of it.

CHAPTER 3

Games

Most children come into Years 3 and 4 keen to participate in games, so it is important to build on this enthusiasm and to develop their understanding and skills. They will have had a range of different experiences of manipulating and using apparatus at Key Stage 1, but it is still important for them to have plenty of opportunities to practise skills individually and in pairs. Large group games activities or scaled down versions of adult games are inappropriate at this stage and the emphasis should be on enabling rather than discouraging experiences.

These units of work concentrate on introducing and developing a variety of games skills using a range of equipment. From individual practise and personal challenges this will naturally lead to small-team games where children can use these skills and tactics to beat or outwit each other.

Many of the games introduced can be adapted to the apparatus and space available and to the children's level of skill and prior experience. Instructions for some warm-up and cool-down games are provided on photocopiable pages 127–31.

These lessons should ideally be taken outside wherever possible so that children will have the opportunity for vigorous activity in a large space in the fresh air.

Colour-coded equipment is recommended for ease of organisation and to enable and encourage children to develop a sense of responsibility for taking out and using, checking and putting away the equipment.

It would be a good idea to have four regular colour groups with a list of names on the classroom wall for ease of reference. Each group can be made responsible for one basket of equipment – collecting it from the PE cupboard, carrying and placing it in the corners of the space to be used. This has a number of advantages:

- The playing area is defined.
- Children are responsibile for the equipment.
- The equipment is dispersed for easier collection (minimising congestion).
- The time spent collecting and returning the equipment is minimised.
- Tidying and checking the equipment at the end of each session is made easier.
- Children are involved in looking after and checking their own equipment and baskets.
- The equipment will be ready for the next class.

Striking and fielding

This unit will help children to develop a range of skills that can be used in invasion games. The lessons will provide opportunities for children to consolidate and extend their experiences of running and jumping; stopping, changing direction and dodging (footwork); carrying and dribbling (travelling with); rolling, bouncing, throwing, striking, kicking and aiming, (sending); catching, stopping and retrieving (receiving).

Invasion games

These lessons will provide a focus on striking and fielding games where the emphasis will be on fielding, bowling and striking skills. With plenty of opportunities to practise these skills, the children can be confident and competent to participate in more complex games in Years 5 and 6.

Invasion games

Invasion games are generally those in which one team invades the territory of another in order to score a goal or cross a line. This could involve running with a ball as in rugby, dribbling or striking a ball as in hockey or soccer or passing a ball as in basketball or netball.

Although each game has its own unique characteristics, the focus is on the generic skills and principles. What is important at this stage is the emphasis on sampling the variety, developing skills and learning to use and apply tactics. Within the unit, children will have the opportunity to travel with, send and receive balls of various sizes, and learn to use and apply tactics while co-operating and competing with a partner or as part of a small team.

The unit is divided into six sessions allowing approximately 30–40 minutes of activity per session. All the work should be taught in the playground wherever possible. It is important that every child has the relevant equipment to practise with before ideas are put into partner work or small-team games. As you become aware of the needs of the class you can adapt the lesson and equipment to suit an individual or a group.

UNIT: Invasion games

Enquiry questions	Learning objectives	Teaching activities	Learning outcomes
How important is footwork?	• Practise different ways of bouncing. • Make up a game that incorporates bouncing in pairs. • Practise rolling and receiving a ball. • Introduce and practise aiming and defending.	Warm-up: walking around the playground, gradually increasing the pace; playing the numbers game, walking them jogging. Development: practising different ways of bouncing; trying to beat their record; practising walking then jogging and bouncing; playing 'Number bouncing'; making up a game of bouncing in pairs; practising rolling a ball to a partner. Games: rolling a ball between two markers to a partner, aiming and defending. Cool-down: jogging then walking around the playground bouncing a ball.	Children: • show good technique when rolling and bouncing a ball • understand the importance of good footwork when defending an area
Can we bounce a ball on the move?	• Practise different ways of bouncing a ball, trying to beat individual records. • Practise and improve the bounce pass on the move. • Practise indicating and moving to receive a pass. • Practise the 'ready' position and develop the ability to move in any direction to receive a ball.	Warm-up: jogging with two beanbags around the playground, running in and out of them. Development: practising different ways of bouncing and adding a challenge; Games: practising bounce passing to a partner; attacking and defending. Cool-down: individually practising different ways of bouncing and catching.	• improve the accuracy of their bounce passes • understand the concept of attacking and defending • indicate their direction and move to receive a bounce pass • make the best use of the space in the playground
How can we use our feet to pass and dribble?	• Practise dribbling a ball with different parts of the feet. • Practise stopping a ball with feet in different ways. • Practise passing and receiving a large ball using feet. • Practise aiming.	Warm-up: jogging slowly around the playground then reducing the area; practising sprinting and jogging. Development: walking around, pushing the ball with the inside then outside of the feet; practising dribbling and stopping the ball; playing 'Stop and go'; dribbling the ball in and out then around the markers; passing the ball to each other using the inside of the foot in pairs; practising stopping and returning; trying different ways of stopping the ball; dribbling the ball between markers and passing it back to a partner who repeats the action; passing the ball to a partner between the skittles. Cool-down: moving around the playground, controlling the ball with feet.	• dribble a ball with both feet • keep control of a ball

UNIT: Invasion games

Enquiry questions	Learning objectives	Teaching activities	Learning outcomes
Can we improve our dribbling skills?	● Practise different ways of dribbling, stopping and changing direction with the ball using feet individually. ● Practise dribbling and passing with a partner.	Warm-up: playing chase. Development: walking then jogging around the playground using the inside then the outside of the feet to dribble; practising different ways to stop, start and change direction with the ball; dribbling the ball around obstacles using each foot in turn; practising dribbling and stopping the ball; in pairs, one dribbling, one shadowing and trying to dispossess; practising passing to a partner. Games: in groups of four, dribbling, passing and intercepting the ball. Cool-down: individually trying to keep the ball in the air with the feet.	● pass a ball accurately
Can we dribble and pass with a Uni-hoc stick	● Practise dribbling with a stick in different directions. ● Practise stopping (receiving) and starting individually and in pairs. ● Practise pushing (sending) the ball with a stick to a partner. ● Combine dribbling and pushing.	Warm-up: jogging around in different directions changing direction quickly; playing 'This way and that'. Development: practising dribbling the ball with a stick, dribbling around markers; practising stopping the ball; in pairs practising pushing the ball to each other. Games: in pairs pushing the ball to each other through two markers like a goal; dribbling the ball around three markers in a line. Cool-down: dribbling the ball forwards, backwards and sideways.	● hold a stick correctly ● keep the ball under control when dribbling ● pass between markers accurately
Can we improve our ball control?	● Practise dribbling, stopping, starting and changing direction, moving a ball with a stick, individually and in a group. ● Practise push-passing a ball using a Uni-hoc stick, on the spot and on the move. ● Practise passing the ball ahead of a partner for them to run onto.	Warm-up: practising dribbling and stopping the ball. Development: individually dribbling the ball around markers; in pairs practising pushing the ball to each other, stopping it before returning it; trying passing to a partner on the move. Games: in threes, practising passing the ball to each other on the move, then two players pass the ball while one tries to intercept. Cool-down: jogging around the playground in different directions, practising the pivot, and continuing jogging.	● improve their dribbling skills ● move into space when playing passing games ● stop the ball with control after dribbling.

Cross-curricular links
Science: making the heart beat faster (pulse work); basic understanding of how the body works during exercise.
PHSE: working and co-operating with others.
Numeracy: keeping score.

Resources
Small, medium and large balls; skittles; beanbags; cones; bands; Uni-hoc or hockey sticks; photocopiable pages 127–31.

Invasion games

(40 mins) How important is footwork?

What you need and preparation

You will need: baskets containing sufficient medium and large balls for one per child; skittles, beanbags or other markers.

Discuss with the children the safety issues involved in working in the playground, and where they are to go.

What to do

(5 mins) Warm-up

Ask the children to walk anywhere in the playground, gradually increasing the pace of the action. Encourage them to look for spaces to move into.

Play a non-elimination version of a numbers game – ask the children to walk round the playground and when you call out a number, the children are to form groups of that number by joining hands in a circle.

Play the game again, but ask the children to jog or run in between the numbers being called.

(15 mins) Development

Tell the children to get either a medium or large ball and to practise different ways of bouncing it (both hands, one hand, alternate hands and so on).

Ask them to see how many bounces they can achieve without stopping. Challenge them with questions such as: *Can you use one hand?* Remind them to start counting again from one if the ball goes astray. Ask: *Can you beat your record?* Let them repeat the exercise, trying to beat that number.

Then see how many bounces they can achieve without stopping with the other hand. Again, repeat, asking them to try to beat their record.

Ask the children to walk around the playground, bouncing the ball, then ask them to try jogging, always keeping control of the ball.

Teach the children the game 'Number bouncing'. When you say *One*, they must walk around the playground, bouncing the ball; when you say *Two*, they must stand still, bouncing the ball;

Learning objectives
- Practise different ways of bouncing.
- Make up a game that incorporates bouncing in pairs.
- Practise rolling and receiving a ball.
- Introduce and practise aiming and defending.

Lesson organisation
Discussion in the classroom; individual and group warm-up; individual and paired development and games; individual cool-down; teacher-led classroom review.

Vocabulary
increasing
decreasing
pace
attack
defend
roll
bounce
stop
sender
receiver

and when you say *Three*, they must run around the playground, bouncing the ball. If some children find it hard performing all three activities, just work on two of them.

Organise the children into pairs and, with one ball between two, ask them to make up a game of bouncing. For example, bouncing to each other standing still or on the move, trying to beat their joint record; bouncing the ball around their partner and then bouncing it to them to do likewise; bouncing the ball alternately on the spot. Encourage them to take fair turns. Some children can be challenged to add an action before they catch the bounced ball, for example a clap or touching the ground.

Move on to ask the children to roll a ball of their choice along the ground to their partner. Remind them that if the sender is rolling the ball with their right hand, their left leg should be in front of their right foot to ensure good balance.

 Games

Ask each pair to keep their ball and get two skittles, beanbags or other markers from the baskets. Ask the pairs to position their markers between them, about two metres apart .

Tell the children to label themselves 'A' and 'B'. Encourage the 'A's to roll the ball between the two markers to their partner, 'B'. Explain that the 'B's then roll the ball back between the targets to 'A'. Encourage the receiver to watch the ball and prepare their hands to receive it. After five goes each, encourage them to make the target area smaller, and ask the senders (those rolling) to move further away from the targets. If this becomes too difficulat, then make the target area larger and ask the senders to move closer to it.

Now tell the pairs to play a different game. 'A' rolls the ball and 'B' has to prevent it from going between the two markers (the goal). Encourage accurate rolling from the sender. The receiver, who must remain in between the markers, should aim to anticipate where the ball is going to arrive and try to stop it before it rolls through the markers. 'B' then rolls the ball to return it to 'A'. Tell them to change over after five goes. Advise them to be ready to move in any direction.

Now ask the pairs to get two more markers from the baskets, so that they each have a 'goal' to attack and defend. Still with one ball between two, both players should roll the ball to try to score a goal in each other's areas (attacking) as well as defend their own. Ask them where and how they should defend the goal.

 Cool-down

Ask the children to put away all the markers, and to choose one ball each. Encourage them to jog, then walk around the playground, bouncing their ball. Ask them to slow down gradually and bounce the ball on the spot.

Finally, ask everyone to return the balls to the baskets.

Classroom review

Ask the children what they felt they did well. Ask them where they stood to receive the ball. *Were you still? Which position helps you to be ready to move in any direction? What were the rules that players had to follow? What helped you to roll accurately?*

Assessing learning outcomes

Do all the children show good technique when rolling and bouncing the ball? Do they understand the importance of good footwork when defending an area? Do the exercises need to be made easier or more difficult for the next lesson? Would it be useful to repeat any or the activities next week?

Invasion games

⏱40 mins Can we bounce a ball on the move?

What you need and preparation

You will need: baskets containing sufficient medium-sized balls for one each; skittles, beanbags or other markers.

Remind the children of the safety issues involved in working in the playground, and where they are to go.

What to do

⏱5 mins Warm-up

Ask each child to take two beanbags from the baskets, and to jog with them freely around the playground. On a given signal (for example *Change*) they are to place their beanbags on the floor and run in and out of the spaces made. On the next signal *Change*, they are to pick up their beanbags and jog around the playground until the next signal. Continue to play like this until their pulses are raised.

⏱20 mins Development

Ask the children to put their beanbags back in the baskets, and to get one ball each. Encourage them to bounce the ball anywhere around them, using two hands, one hand or alternate hands.

Challenge them to bounce the ball in different ways (see Diagram 1):
● high into the air and catch it
● on the spot and then on the move
● on the move, keeping it to the side of the body.

Ask them to choose and add a challenge (for example clapping hands before catching the ball, moving sideways, using alternate hands). Prompt them by asking: *Can you bounce the ball high and low and still keep control? Can you beat your record?* Encourage them all to practise bouncing on the move. *Can you move in different directions?*

Ask the children to get into pairs, labelling themselves 'A' and 'B', and stand three to four metres away from their partners with one ball between two. Encourage them to pass the ball

Learning objectives
● Practise different ways of bouncing a ball, trying to beat individual records.
● Practise and improve the bounce pass on the move.
● Practise indicating and moving to receive a pass.
● Practise the 'ready' position and develop the ability to move in any direction to receive a ball.

Lesson organisation
Discussion in the classroom; individual and group warm-up; individual, paired and group games; individual cool-down; teacher-led classroom review.

Vocabulary
anticipate
alternate
bounce
pick up
dummy
intercept
consecutive

Diagram 1

Invasion games

to each other so that it bounces once about half-way between them. Explain that the ball needs to be pushed downwards and forwards with both hands (like a chest pass) as the bounce pass is made.

This time, 'A' bounces the ball first to one side and then to the other side of their partner for them to catch. Encourage 'B' to return to the middle spot (opposite their partner) each time after returning the ball to 'A'. Demonstrate this with one pair. After five goes, ask the partners to swap over, to ensure fair turns.

Now encourage 'B' to signal which side they want their partner to bounce the ball for them to catch by indicating quickly with their hand. 'A' watches and passes ahead of 'B' for them to catch and return. Emphasise co-operating with their partner, and challenge the children to count the number of successful passes. Again, remind them to swap over, to ensure fair turns.

Games

Ask each pair to join another pair, with one large ball between four. Help them to position themselves in a grid or specified area (such as a sixth of the netball court). One pair bounce passes the ball to each other, trying to make five passes without the other pair intercepting. Each pair scores a point if they make five passes without interception. After five passes, the other pair start with the ball. Ask the children what rules they need to make (for when the ball goes out of the area and when one player touches another and so on). Can they help their partners by indicating where they want the ball to be passed to?

Cool-down

Ask the children to get one ball each to practise different ways of bouncing and catching. They could, for example, bounce the ball moving forwards, sideways and backwards; bounce the ball on the ground as high as possible and catch it before it lands.

Classroom review

Ask the children what they think they were successful at. What strategies could be employed to deceive the defender (dummy pass)? Did anyone anticipate the direction of the pass and get behind the ball to catch it?

Assessing learning outcomes

How accurate are the children's bounce passes? Do all the children understand the concept of attacking and defending? Are they able to indicate their direction and move to receive the bounce pass? Did they make the best use of the space in the playground for the paired activities?

(40 mins) How can we use our feet to pass and dribble?

What you need and preparation

You will need: large (Size 3) balls; markers.

Discuss in the classroom the activities planned for the lesson and where the children are to go in the playground.

What to do

(5 mins) Warm-up

Ask the children to jog slowly around the playground and then in a smaller area (such as a third of a netball court). On the signal *Fast*, encourage them to sprint, and on the signal *Jog*, make sure they return to jogging. Repeat this combination five times. Encourage clear changes of speed and direction and movement into open spaces.

(22 mins) Development

Ask the children to get one large ball each from the baskets. Tell them to walk around the playground or a specified grid, pushing the ball with the inside of their feet. Encourage them to dribble the ball around the playground, keeping it as close to their feet as possible. Emphasise that you want them to use both feet. Then ask them to try this dribbling action using the outside of the feet.

Ask the children to return to dribbling around the playground, using the inside of their feet. On the signal *Stop*, ask them to stop the ball from moving by placing one foot on top of it. On the signal *Go*, tell them to continue dribbling the ball. When dribbling, advise them to keep the ball as close to the feet as possible, which will make it easier to stop on the given signal.

Then encourage the children to play this 'stop and go' game, but using only the outside of their feet.

Ask the children to place about 30 markers around the playground. Encourage them to dribble their ball around the space, but when they reach a marker, to go right around it and then move on. See how many markers they can dribble around in 30, 60 or 90 seconds. Let them choose whether they use the inside or outside of their feet.

Now ask the children to get into pairs, with one ball between two, and to stand ready three to four metres apart. Encourage them to pass the ball to each other using the inside of the foot. Explain that the receiver must stop the ball before returning it. Encourage them to try different ways of stopping the ball.

Still in pairs, ask the children to label themselves 'A' and 'B' and place five markers in a row. Ask the 'A's to dribble in between the markers. When they reach the end, they dribble back again between the markers and pass the ball to their partner, who then repeats the exercise.

(8 mins) Games

Tell the pairs to put away the markers and get two skittles, so that they have two skittles and one ball between two. Ask the 'A's to pass the ball to the 'B's between the skittles. The 'B's must then stop the ball and return it to the 'A's between the two skittles. Encourage accuracy and challenge them to co-operate to beat their record of successful passes and returns.

(5 mins) Cool-down

Ask the children to return all the skittles and markers to the baskets, and to get one ball each. Encourage them to move around the playground, controlling the ball with their feet. On the signal *Stop*, ask them to stop the ball and then move on.

Learning objectives
- Practise dribbling a ball with different parts of the feet.
- Practise stopping the ball with feet in different ways.
- Practise passing and receiving a large ball using feet.
- Practise aiming.

Lesson organisation
Brief classroom discussion; individual warm-up; individual and paired activities; individual cool-down; teacher-led classroom review.

Vocabulary
dribbling
passing
stopping
sprinting
jogging

Classroom review

Ask the class how they could make the passing activity (through the skittles) more challenging. *Which foot did you find it easier to dribble and pass with?*

Assessing learning outcomes

Are the childrenable to dribble the ball with both feet? Can they keep control of the ball? Were the pairs appropriately grouped in terms of skill level?

(40 mins) Can we improve our dribbling skills?

Learning objectives
● Practise different ways of dribbling, stopping and changing direction with the ball using the feet individually.
● Practise dribbling and passing with a partner.

Lesson organisation
Teacher-led classroom discussion; group warm-up; individual, paired and group activities; individual cool-down; teacher-led classroom review.

Vocabulary
dribble
pass
possession
shadow
tackle
shield
defend
intercept

What you need and preparation

You will need: large and medium balls; bands; skittles or cones; chalk.

Discuss key points of passing from the previous lesson; ensure that the children are clear what space they need to work in.

What to do

(5 mins) Warm-up
Choose four children from the class to wear bands. Ask these four (the chasers) to attempt to catch the other children (the free runners). Explain that when a chaser touches a free runner, that person takes the band and becomes a chaser whilst the other person becomes a free runner.

(15 mins) Development
Ask the children to get one ball each, and to walk or jog around the playground using the inside then the outside of their feet, keeping the ball under control. Encourage them to practise different ways to stop, start and change direction with the ball.

Ask the children to put beanbags, skittles or other markers around the playground or in a grid area. Ask them to dribble the ball along the ground, and when they meet an obstacle, to push the ball past it with the outside of their foot. Encourage them to use both feet.

Ask the children to dribble the ball in control around the playground or grid and, on your signal *Stop*, to stop the ball by placing their foot on top of it. Once the ball has been stopped, each child then passes to another person and continues to dribble their 'new' ball around the playground or grid.

In pairs, ask one player, 'A', to dribble the ball with their feet, and 'B' to shadow their partner, trying to take over the ball if it goes astray. Stress that they are not allowed to tackle. 'A' tries to shield the ball from 'B' as they move around the space. Ensure fair turns and emphasise that no contact is allowed.

Now practise passing in twos on the move. 'A' passes to 'B' who runs on to the ball, controls it and dribbles it forward a little before passing it to 'A'. Emphasise to the children that they should be running onto the ball.

(15 mins) Games
Ask the children to get into groups of four, and to get one ball and four markers per group. The first person dribbles the ball between the equally spaced markers. When they reach the end line, they turn around and pass the ball to the second person who then dribbles between the markers. The activity finishes when the last person dribbles between the markers and passes the end line. Encourage the children to use both feet when dribbling. Challenge them to try this activity again, but with the markers irregularly placed.

Now ask the groups to mark out an area (either using lines already on the playground, or with chalk). Ensuring that they stay within the grid, nominate three members of each group to pass the ball between each other whilst the remaining member attempts to intercept it. Encourage the three passers to try to keep possession for five consecutive passes. When either five consecutive passes have been made or the defender intercepts, change over to ensure that everyone has a go at being the defender.

⑤ Cool-down
Ask the children to put away all the equipment and get one ball each. Challenge them to try to keep the ball in the air using their feet only, continually trying to beat their own record.

To finish, ask the children to dribble their ball slowly sideways and to put it in its basket.

Classroom review
Ask the children what skills they require to keep the ball under control when dribbling. How many times could they keep the ball in the air without it touching the floor?

Assessing learning outcomes
Can all the children pass the ball accurately? Were the groups in the partner activities appropriately set?

④⓪ Can we dribble and pass with a Uni-hoc stick?

What you need and preparation
You will need: Uni-hoc or hockey sticks; small balls; cones, skittles or beanbags.

In the classroom, discuss with the children the safety implications involved when using a Uni-hoc or hockey stick (for example *Don't raise the stick above waist height* and *use two hands on the stick at all times*).

What to do

⑥ Warm-up
In a marked out area, ask the children to jog around in different directions using all the spaces. On the signal *Change*, ask them to change direction quickly.

With all the children facing you, ask them to play 'This way and that', encouraging them to be in the 'ready' position to start with. When you say *This way*, they run to the left, and when you say *That way*, they run to the right. Make sure that they run towards the indicated line (ensure this is not near a wall or any protruding areas), but keep changing the commands to keep them changing direction. Encourage them to return to the ready position facing you whenever they can.

⑮ Development
Ask the children to get a small ball and a Uni-hoc or hockey stick each. Encourage them to move around the playground, pushing the ball along the ground and keeping it close to the stick. Encourage them to hold the stick with the left hand at the top and the right hand half-way down (reverse for left handers), and to push and steer the ball rather than hit it.

Put markers or cones around the playground. Ask the children to dribble the ball and when they reach a marker to go right around it and then dribble their ball to another obstacle. See how many markers each child can go round in 30 seconds. Encourage them to move their feet as they do this and to practise stopping the ball to keep it under control.

Learning objectives
● Practise dribbling with a stick in different directions.
● Practise stopping (receiving) and starting individually and in pairs.
● Practise pushing (sending) the ball with a stick to a partner.
● Combine dribbling and pushing.

Lesson organisation
Classroom discussion; individual warm-up; individual and paired activities; individual cool-down; teacher-led classroom review.

Vocabulary
pushing
sending
dribbling
tapping
steering

Invasion games

Organise the children into pairs and ask them to put one ball away so that they have one stick each and one small ball between two. Encourage the the senders to push the ball to their partners with their sticks, while the receivers stop it with control and send it back. Emphasise that this is a pushing and not a hitting action and encourage everyone to start the action with the stick close to the ball (see Diagram 2) .

Diagram 2

*After full
tu width
point out a
line
one will
dribble
to the
point &
pass the
ball
then
jog
back
the other
repects
could add targets*

✳ As the children become more competent, encourage them to move further apart from their partners. For the stopping action, advise them to face their partner and the incoming ball and to keep their stick upright in front of their feet. *moving back*

(14 mins) Games
Ask the pairs to stand four metres apart, and to put two markers on the ground between them. Encourage them to push the ball through the space between the markers to one another, stopping the ball before returning it. Ask them how they can make this harder or easier (by making the 'goal' narrower or wider).

Then ask the children to collect another marker and spread the three markers out in a line. Encourage the children to dribble the ball between the markers and then pass the ball to their partners, who then do the same. See how quickly they can go in and out of the markers and still keep control of the ball. Encourage them to keep practising this, and then to try dribbling the ball right around each marker.

(5 mins) Cool-down
Ask the children to put away all the markers and to have one small ball and a stick each. Encourage them to practise dribbling, in control, around the playground, forwards, backwards and sideways.

Classroom review

Ask the children how they could make the obstacle game between the markers easier or harder. Ask them how their bodies felt at the end of the lesson. *Were you out of breath or tired? Was your heart beating faster?*

Assessing learning outcomes

Are the children holding the stick correctly? Are they keeping the ball under control when dribbling? Are they accurate in their passing between markers?

40 mins Can we improve our ball control?

What you need and preparation

You will need: Uni-hoc or hockey sticks; small balls; markers – cones, beanbags or skittles.

In the classroom, discuss with the children the key points from the previous lesson, especially the correct ways of holding the stick and pushing the ball.

What to do

6 mins Warm-up

Ask the children to take a Uni-hoc or hockey stick and a small ball each. Let them practise dribbling the ball anywhere in the playground, keeping the ball close to their stick. Remind them of the way to hold the stick and emphasise steering rather than hitting the ball. On your *Stop* signal, tell them to stop and control the ball, then move on.

This time on the *Stop* signal, encourage them to stop the ball and move onto someone else's ball and continue dribbling.

20 mins Development

Ask the children to place cones, markers, beanbags and skittles freely around the playground. Then encourage them to dribble their ball around as many markers as they can in 60 seconds, keeping the ball under control.

Now ask the children to form pairs. Tell them to replace one ball so that each person has a stick and there is one ball between two. Ask them to find a space and, standing six metres apart, to practise pushing the ball to each other, stopping it before pushing it back to their partner.

Then ask them to try this on the move, passing the ball a little ahead of their partner for them to run onto. Repeat this several times.

10 mins Games

Put the children into groups of three, labelling them 'A', 'B' and 'C'. Ask them to pass to each other within a specified area (such as a sixth of a netball court) keeping on the move, stopping and controlling the ball before pushing it to one of the other players.

Next, in the same area, ask the 'A's and 'B's to pass the ball between them, while the 'C's try to intercept the ball once it has been passed. Explain that each group must stay in their area and no tackling is allowed. Change roles after five consecutive passes are made or the ball is intercepted. Encourage the children to move into a space to receive the ball.

4 mins Cool-down

Ask the children to put all of the equipment away, and then to jog around the playground in different directions without touching anyone. On the signal *Stop*, ask them to stop with one foot in front of the other in a balanced and controlled position. Then ask them to pivot, keeping the back foot on the ground, and jog off in a different direction.

Classroom review

Ask the children what is the correct way to hold a hockey stick when dribbling. Ask them what is the easiest way of stopping a moving ball when it is coming towards them.

Assessing learning outcomes

Have the children's dribbling skills improved? Did they move into space when playing the passing games? Were they able to stop their ball with control after dribbling?

Learning objectives
● Practise dribbling, stopping, starting and changing direction, moving a ball with a stick, individually and in a group.
● Practise push-passing a ball using a Uni-hoc stick, on the spot and on the move.
● Practise passing the ball ahead of their partner for them to run onto.

Lesson organisation
Classroom discussion; individual warm-up; individual and paired development; group games; individual cool-down; teacher-led classroom review.

Vocabulary
dribble
push
stop
steer
pivot

Striking and fielding

This unit of work looks at some ways of developing knowledge, skills and understanding for children to participate in striking and fielding activities. Children will spend some time practising and consolidating skills covered previously in these strands at Key Stage 1, for example rolling, bouncing, throwing, catching, retrieving a ball and using a bat.

Children will be taught how to position themselves to collect, stop or intercept a ball and return it accurately, and to hit a ball accurately and into spaces so that they can score runs.

The unit is divided into six lessons, allowing approximately 30–40 minutes of activity per lesson. All activities are best suited to the playground. It is important that every child has the opportunity to practise individually before they play in a group or a small-team game.

UNIT: Striking and fielding

Enquiry questions	Learning objectives	Teaching activities	Learning outcomes
What are the best ways to catch a ball?	● Practise bouncing and catching in different ways, trying to beat personal records. ● Practise bouncing and catching on the move. ● Practise running to field and pick up a moving ball in different ways. ● Make up a bouncing, catching and aiming game in pairs.	Warm-up: practising running, jumping and landing, making different shapes; bouncing in different ways trying to beat personal records. Development: bouncing and catching a ball low and high; throwing and catching on the spot and on the move; in pairs bouncing a ball to each other; bouncing a ball for a partner to chase and catch. Games: making up a game that includes bouncing, catching and aiming. Cool-down: throwing and catching.	Children: ● catch a ball with both hands ● move to catch a ball
How do we field a rolling ball?	● Practise catching in different ways, trying to beat personal records. ● Practise chasing, fielding, stopping and returning a rolling ball. ● Practise aiming a rolling ball through a target or goal. ● Practise with a partner and a group to stop a rolling ball.	Warm-up: running and leaping; rolling a ball and chasing it; practising different ways of stopping and picking up a ball. Development: catching in different ways; using the hand as a bat to tap the ball up; rolling and stopping the ball in pairs; rolling a ball between markers and fielding it. Games: rolling a ball in threes with a fourth player intercepting. Cool-down: bouncing and passing a ball around the body.	● catch a ball when it is thrown in the air ● improve accuracy when rolling a ball between markers
How do we bowl underarm?	● Practise changing direction quickly. ● Practise rolling and stopping a ball at speed. ● Practise underarm bowling. ● Practise striking a ball with a bat. ● Co-operate in pairs to play a game.	Warm-up: jogging in different directions; playing 'Chase and change'. Development: rolling and chasing a ball and picking it up in different ways; throwing the ball underarm for a partner to catch; balancing a ball on a bat while walking; tapping the ball into the air. Games: bowling, batting and catching co-operating in pairs. Cool-down: running, jogging then walking.	● return the ball to their partner accurately with a bat ● co-operate in pairs
Can we improve the accuracy of our bowling and batting?	● Practise changing direction quickly. ● Improve underarm bowling for accuracy. ● Practise striking a ball with a bat, individually and with a partner.	Warm-up: side-stepping in both directions; playing 'Chase and change'; throwing a ball in the air and catching alternately with a partner. Development: bowling in pairs; individually tapping the ball continuously upwards while moving; bouncing a ball into a hoop for partner to hit back to catch. Games: in twos, practising batting, bowling and catching. Cool-down: bouncing or throwing and catching and to trying to beat personal record.	● improve the accuracy of their bowling actions ● catch a partner's ball

UNIT: Striking and fielding

Enquiry questions	Learning objectives	Teaching activities	Learning outcomes
Can we play rota-rounders?	● Practise and improve the hitting action. ● Practise throwing a ball overarm. ● Introduce different roles in a game – bowler, fielder and batter.	Warm-up: walking and running fast for ten seconds alternately; bouncing or throwing and catching a ball. Development: throwing the ball overarm and running to collect it; practising underarm bowling; practising ways of throwing and catching with a partner; throwing the ball overarm for a partner to catch; practising bowling, hitting and catching in pairs. Games: in fours playing rota-rounders. Cool-down: practising throwing and catching in different ways.	● strike the ball accurately ● co-operate to rotate as a group
Can we strike and field better?	● Practise throwing overarm into a target. ● Practise hitting into a space to avoid fielders. ● Practise working together as a team of fielders.	Warm-up: skipping, pushing up into the air; bouncing and catching on the move in different directions, using both hands. Development: throwing the ball into the air and catching it; throwing into a space and collecting it; in pairs throwing underarm; throwing overarm into a hoop to a partner; throwing overarm for a partner to catch. Games: playing rota-rounders, scoring runs. Cool-down: throwing or tapping the ball into the air.	● judge where batters are going to hit the ball when they are fielding ● hit the ball into space, away from fielders when they are batting.

Cross-curricular links
PSHE: working and sharing with others; co-operating as a team.
Maths: counting, looking at shapes and size; keeping score.
Science: being aware of pulse raising, heart rates.

Resources
Small and medium balls; hoops; bats; markers (skittles, cones and/or beanbags); padder/tennis bats; a whistle; photocopiable pages 126–31.

Striking and fielding

(35 mins) What are the best ways to catch?

What you need and preparation

You will need: a variety of balls, mainly medium and small.

In the classroom, go over the main teaching points for catching and throwing with the children – that they keep their eyes on the ball, and catch with their hands cupped together.

What to do

(5 mins) Warm-up

Ask the children to run anywhere in the playground and, on your signal *Jump*, jump up in the air and make a shape. Tell them, on landing, to run again and this time make a different shape. Encourage them by asking: *Can you try wide shapes and narrow shapes in the air?*

Ask them to get a small ball each, and to bounce it on the spot in a space. Ask the children to throw the ball up in the air and let it bounce, then catch it with two cupped hands. Encourage them to count as they do this and then try to beat their record. Then invite them to bounce the ball and catch it whilst on the move, using both hands or one hand. Can they use their right and their left hand to bounce the ball?

(16 mins) Development

Ask the children to bounce the ball near the ground and catch it, then to bounce it as high as they can, letting it bounce again before catching it. Ask them to think of and then try some other ways they could bounce and catch the ball. Encourage them to keep practising and improve their technique. Prompt them with: *Can you beat your record?*

Now tell the children to throw the ball into the air a little way and to practise catching it before it bounces. Emphasise that they should have their hands ready and be watching the ball. Ask them to count how many catches they can make without the ball dropping and then to try to beat their record. See if they can do this on the move.

Ask the children to get into pairs, with one ball between two. Ask them to stand three to four metres apart, and for one partner ('A') to bounce the ball to the other ('B'), who must catch it. Tell them that the ball should be caught at around chest height, and to bear this in mind when bouncing the ball to each other. Encourage the children to watch the ball and be ready to move to catch it.

Now tell the pairs to start standing side by side, facing the space where 'B' was standing for the last practice. Explain tha Player 'A' bounces the ball into the same space and 'B' runs forward to catch it or pick it up. 'B' bounces the ball back to 'A' and runs back to 'A' ready for them to bounce the ball again. Ask the players to change roles every three bounces.

(10 mins) Games

Ask the pairs to make up a game that includes bouncing, catching and aiming, using one ball and one or two hoops. Ask them to think about how they can ensure fair turns.

(4 mins) Cool-down

Ask the children to get out one ball each for individual practice. Encourage them to throw it in the air and see if they can clap before they catch it. Can they clap more than once? Encourage them to keep trying to beat their own record of claps.

Learning objectives
● Practise bouncing and catching in different ways, trying to beat personal records.
● Practise bouncing and catching on the move.
● Practise running to field and pick up a moving ball in different ways.
● Make up a bouncing, catching and aiming game in pairs.

Lesson organisation
Classroom discussion; individual warm-up; individual and paired activities and games; individual cool-down; teacher-led classroom review.

Vocabulary
catch
bounce
on the move
on the spot
accurate
target

Striking and fielding

Classroom review

Ask the children what they need to remember when they catch a ball. *What do you need to do with your hands? What do you need to do with your feet when catching a ball?*

Assessing learning outcomes

Are the children able to catch a ball with both hands? Are they able to move to catch the ball?

35 mins How do we field a rolling ball?

Learning objectives
● Practise catching in different ways, trying to beat personal records.
● Practise chasing, fielding, stopping and returning a rolling ball.
● Practise aiming a rolling ball through a target or goal.
● Practise with a partner and a group to stop a rolling ball.

Lesson organisation
Classroom discussion; individual warm-up; individual, paired and small group activities; individual cool-down; teacher-led classroom review.

What you need and preparation

You will need: small and medium balls; markers; hoops. Ensure there is enough space and equipment for the rolling and fielding activities (see Development and Games).

In the classroom, remind the children about how to catch from the previous lesson.

What to do

4 mins Warm up

Ask the children to run anywhere in the playground and, on your signal *Jump*, to leap in the air. Invite them to practise landing and running on for several minutes until their pulse is raised.

Then ask the children to get a small ball each. Ask them to roll it away into a large space and run to collect it several times. Ask them to practise different ways of stopping and picking up the ball.

16 mins Development
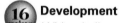
With a ball each, ask the children to try out the following activities, counting how many catches they can make before the ball goes astray:
● Throw or bounce the ball in the air and catch it with both hands.
● Throw or bounce the ball in the air and catch it with one hand.
● Throw the ball in the air, turn around and catch it with both hands or one hand.
● Throw the ball in the air, touch the ground and catch the ball before it bounces.

Now ask everyone to try using their hand as a bat as they tap the ball up into the air. Can they use both sides of their hand?

Organise the children into pairs to practise rolling the ball to each other. Emphasise that they should be watching the ball and have their hands ready. Advise them to scoop the ball up quickly, positioning their body behind the ball. Encourage them to keep low as they practise gathering the ball and to step forward on their left foot if they are rolling the ball with their right hand. Challenge them to return the ball to their partner as quickly as possible.

Vocabulary
run
collect
field
roll
target
goal
accurate

Ask the pairs to get one ball and two markers between two. Ask them to label themselves 'A' and 'B' and to lay out their markers like a goal between them. Help them to try the following activities:
● 'A' rolls the ball between the two markers to 'B', who has to field the ball and roll it back between the two markers to return it. The markers can be put closer together to make it harder to aim at or further apart to make it easier. Look for accuracy.

● 'A' rolls the ball between the two markers and 'B' returns it by bouncing or throwing the ball back to 'A'. Make sure the children take turns to do this.

● With an extra marker placed beside the original goal in a line, ask 'A' to roll the ball through one of the goals for 'B' to field. 'B' does the same as they roll to return it to 'A'. Suggest that they can score a point for each ball accurately rolled and picked up. Encourage them to see how many points they can score in a set time. Ask them how they can tell which goal their partner might roll the ball through and how they can be ready to move to pick it up.

(10 mins) Games

Ask each pair to join another pair in a space and for three of them to stand in a triangle. The fourth player starts the game in the middle. The aim is for the three players to roll the ball to each other without the middle player intercepting the ball. If the middle player stops or gathers the ball, they change places with the player who rolled it. Ensure that they each player has fair opportunities to be in the middle. (This may mean specifying a change-over time.)

(5 mins) Cool-down

Ask the children to put away all the markers, and get a small or medium ball each. Encourage them to bounce the ball around their body while keeping their feet still. Then ask them to pass the ball from hand to hand around their body, quickly then slowly. Finally, ask everyone to put the balls away.

Classroom review

Ask the children to describe the most efficient way to stop a ball that is rolling towards them. Ask how accurate they were when rolling the ball between the targets. *What helped you to be ready?*

Assessing learning outcomes

Can all the children catch the ball when it is thrown in the air? How accurate are they at rolling the ball between the markers?

(35 mins) How do we bowl underarm?

What you need and preparation

You will need: bats – preferably padder/tennis-type bats with a short handle; small balls; hoops; markers – cones or skittles; a whistle (optional). NB. To enable the children to strike the ball successfully it is important that the bats have a broad face, so *not* rounders bats.

In the classroom, remind the children of the need to be aware of each other and the space when using bats and balls.

Learning objectives
● Practise changing direction quickly.
● Practise rolling and stopping a ball at speed.
● Practise underarm bowling.
● Practise striking a ball with a bat.
● Co-operate in pairs to play a game.

Lesson organisation
Classroom discussion; individual and paired warm-up and activities; individual cool-down; teacher-led classroom review.

What to do

(5 mins) Warm-up

Ask the children to jog around the playground using different directions. Then ask them to get into pairs and label themselves 'A' and 'B' to play 'Chase and change'. Ask the 'A's to be the chasers and to chase the 'B's around the playground starting one metre apart. Explain to the children that on your signal *Change*, they change

Striking and fielding

Vocabulary
chase
change
roll
stop
scoop
chest height
underarm throw
bowling action

roles so that 'B's chase 'A's. If they touch their partner before the command *Change*, they change over straightaway. Ensure that all the children have several opportunities to chase and be chased.

15 mins Development

Ask the children to collect a ball each and to practise on their own, rolling their ball into a space and chasing to collect it. Encourage them all to try running alongside their ball and scooping it up, and running past their ball, turning and crouching to stop it with two hands. (See Diagram 3.)

Diagram 3

In pairs, with one ball between two, ask the children to practise throwing the ball underarm for their partner to catch (standing about three metres apart). Ask the catcher to help their partner by having their hands ready about chest height and to practise 'giving' on catching the ball. Encourage the partner who is throwing to aim for the hands, following through with their fingers in that direction. Check that the leg opposite to the throwing arm is forward. (See Diagram 4.)

Encourage the pairs to co-operate and count how many accurate, caught passes they can make before you stay *Stop*. Emphasise that accuracy is important when bowling in a game. Let everyone try again and see if they can beat that number.

Diagram 4

Now ask the children to get a bat and a small ball each from the baskets and to balance the ball on the bat whilst they move around the playground individually. In a space, ask them to tap the ball into the air, let it bounce on the ground, and then tap it into the air again. Encourage them to see how many times they can do this and then to try to beat that record.

12 mins Games

In pairs, with one bat and one ball between two, ask the children to take turns to bat and to catch. Ask them what might be fair (waiting until someone is out or having a set number of turns). Encourage them to change over after four goes. One player throws the ball underarm towards their partner's bat, allowing it to bounce well in front of their partner. The partner watches the bounce and then, standing sideways, tries to hit the ball back towards the thrower for them to catch after a bounce. Prompt the children to improve and keep count: *How many in a row can you catch?* See if they can co-operate to count successful catches and keep trying to beat their record.

Some children could try bowling the ball without a bounce, aiming for their partner's bat. The batter tries to hit the ball for their partner to catch after a bounce or, if possible, without a bounce. How can they help each other to do this? Can they catch as many? How will they ensure fair turns?

3 mins Cool-down

Ask the children to put away all the equipment, and then run around the playground. On a given signal (such as *Jog* or a blow on your whistle), tell them to change to jogging. On the second signal (for example *Walk* or two whistle blows), they should change to walking.

Classroom review

Ask the children about the different ways in which they tried to stop a moving ball.

Assessing learning outcomes

Are the children able to return the ball to their partner accurately with their bat? Are they able to co-operate in pairs?

35 mins Can we improve our bowling and batting?

What you need and preparation

You will need: bats; small balls; hoops; markers – cones or skittles.

In the classroom beforehand, remind the children of the underarm bowling action and the sideways batting stance that they have been practising.

What to do

5 mins Warm-up

To begin, ask the children to slide-step around the space in both directions. Remind them to be aware of where they are going and to look for spaces.

Go on to play 'Chase and change' in pairs. Tell the children to collect a small ball between two and to practise throwing it in the air and catching it alternately on the spot. Then ask them to try to do this as they walk along.

12 mins Development

Still in pairs, with one ball between two, ask the children to practise bowling the ball to their partner as accurately as they can (throwing underarm, aiming between hip and shoulder height). Challenge them to count how many accurate passes they can make together out of ten bowls. Can they beat that record?

Ask the children to get a bat and a small ball each from the baskets and to practise tapping the ball into the air and letting it bounce on the ground. Challenge them to see how many times they can do this successfully and then to try to beat that record. Let them have several practices, then ask them to try hitting the ball continuously upwards while moving slowly around the playground.

Now tell the children to form pairs again and to put away one bat and one ball and collect one hoop between two, so that they have one bat, one ball and one hoop between them. Ask one child from each pair to bounce the ball into the hoop and their partner to hit the ball back for the sender to catch (with or without a bounce). Ensure all the children are having several turns at sending and hitting.

14 mins Games

In the same pairs, with one bat and one ball (putting the hoop away), ask the children to take turns to bat and to bowl and catch, changing over after every four goes. Remind them to stand sideways and to try to hit the ball back towards the thrower for them to catch after a bounce. Then encourage them to catch the ball without a bounce. Emphasise that they should be co-operating to do this.

Then encourage them to try bowling the ball without a bounce, aiming for their partner's bat. Encourage them to aim carefully and think about how hard they are throwing by asking: *Can the batter still return the ball for the bowler to catch? How can you help each other to do this? How many can you catch in a row?*

Learning objectives
● Practise running and changing direction quickly.
● Improve underarm bowling for accuracy.
● Practise striking a ball with a bat individually, and with a partner.

Lesson organisation
Classroom discussion; individual and paired warm-up and activities; individual cool-down; teacher-led classroom review.

Vocabulary
chase
change
underarm throw
bowling action

4 mins **Cool-down**
With the bats away and a ball each, ask the children to practise bouncing or throwing and catching and to try to beat their record.

Classroom review
Ask the children to talk about how they helped each other to hit and catch the ball. How could they do this another time?

Assessing learning outcomes
How accurate are the children's bowling actions? Can they catch their partner's ball?

35 mins Can we play rota-rounders?

Learning objectives
● Improve hitting and improve the hitting action.
● Practise throwing a ball overarm.
● Introduce different roles in a game – bowler, fielder and batter.

Lesson organisation
Classroom discussion; individual warm-up; paired and group activities; individual cool-down; teacher-led classroom review.

Vocabulary
chase
change
underarm throw
bowling action
overarm throw

What you need and preparation
You will need: bats; small balls; hoops; markers – cones or skittles; a whistle (optional).
In the classroom, remind children of the underarm bowling action and the sideways batting stance.

What to do
6 mins **Warm-up**
Ask the children to walk around the playground and, on a given signal (for example a whistle blow or the command *Fast*), to run as fast as possible on the spot for ten seconds and then move on.

Tell them to collect a ball and practise bouncing or throwing and catching the ball, trying to beat their record. Ask them all to practise throwing the ball high into the air and catching it. Let them practise this several times, counting their consecutive successes and trying to improve their record.

10 mins **Development**
Ask the children to practise throwing the ball overarm into a big space and then running to collect it. Make sure that they are using the space and looking before they throw.

In pairs, with one ball between two, ask the children to practise underarm bowling. Ask them to try other ways of throwing and catching with a partner. Select a pair throwing overarm to demonstrate the action, then ask all the children to practise throwing the ball overarm for their partners to catch.

Ask one child from each pair to collect a bat for practice of underarm bowling, hitting and catching in pairs.

15 mins **Games**
Ask each pair to join another pair and to put some equipment away so that they have one bat and one small ball per group of four. Ask the children within each group to number themselves 1, 2, 3 and 4 and to arrange themselves as follows (see Diagram 5):

Striking and fielding

1 – bowler
2 – fielder
3 – batter
4 – fielder.

Hoops can be used to provide a base for the bowler and batter if required.

Explain how the game works. The bowler sends the ball underarm for the batter to hit after it has bounced. The batter then tries to hit the ball for one of the fielders to catch. The fielder returns the ball to the bowler who then bowls another ball. Every player has four goes and then moves on to the next position. The group can count how many catches they can make as a group. Encourage the batter to stand sideways on and to direct the ball to one of the fielders.

Diagram 5

 Cool-down
Ask the children to put all the equipment away, and to get a ball each. Encourage them to throw and catch it in as many different ways as possible.

Classroom review
Ask the children how they tried, when they were batting, to help the fielders to catch the ball. Did they hit carefully, and aim?

Assessing learning outcomes
Are the children able to strike the ball accurately? Do they co-operate to rotate as a group?

35 mins Can we strike and field better?

What you need and preparation
You will need: bats; small balls; hoops; markers – beanbags, cones or skittles.

In the classroom, remind children of the overarm throwing action and the sideways batting stance. Remind them that they need to be aware of each other and the space when using bats and balls. Discuss the need for those who are batting to strike the ball away from other groups.

What to do
 Warm-up
Ask the children to skip around the playground, gradually lifting their knees more and pushing up into the air as they do this.

Ask them to collect a ball each and to practise bouncing and catching it on the move. When you say *Change*, tell them to continue bouncing, but to move in a different direction. Then challenge them to try this using their other hand.

Learning objectives
● Practise throwing overarm into a target.
● Practise hitting into a space to avoid fielders.
● Practise working together as a team of fielders.

Lesson organisation
Classroom discussion; individual and paired warm-up; individual and pair activities; games in fours; individual cool-down; teacher-led classroom review.

Striking and fielding

Vocabulary
underarm throw
bowling action
overarm throw
chase and collect

Development

11 mins Ask the children to practise throwing the ball into the air and catching it and then throwing into a space and chasing to collect it.

In pairs, with one ball between two, ask the children to practise throwing underarm to their partner. Remind them to be as accurate as they can.

Now ask them to collect one hoop between two and to stand, with the hoop in between them, at least six metres apart. Ask one of them to throw the ball overarm into the hoop and their partner to catch or collect it. As soon as the partner has the ball, they should try to aim overarm into the hoop for the first sender to collect. Practise this several times, reminding the children to try to think of ways of improving the accuracy of the throw. Can they help their partner? What could they say that might help? Can they check that their partner has the opposite foot to the throwing arm forward?

Ask the children to put the hoops away and to stand a little further apart to practise throwing the ball overarm for their partner to catch. Encourage them as they practise by asking questions such as: *How many throws can you catch without the ball dropping? Can you beat your record?*

Games

16 mins Ask the children to get into groups of four with one bat, one small ball, a hoop (for the batter to stand in) and a marker (beanbag, cone or skittle). As before (see page 87), ask the groups to number themselves 1, 2, 3 and 4 and to arrange themselves to bowl, bat or field. Place the marker about three metres to the right of the batting position. The bowler bowls underarm and this time, the batter tries to direct the ball into a space to *avoid* the fielders. The fielders have to run to retrieve the ball and return it to the bowler.

Once they have all practised three or four times in each position, the children can try to score runs when they are the batter. Explain that after striking the ball (or missing it) they run around the marker and back to their place to score each run. The bowler shouts *Stop* when they receive the ball in the hoop to stop the batter running.

Cool-down

4 mins Ask the children to put all the equipment away and to get a ball each and practise throwing it or tapping it into the air to catch. Can they beat any of their records?

Classroom review

Ask the children how they helped their partner to throw accurately overarm. What did they say that helped?

Assessing learning outcomes

Were the fielders able to judge where the batters were going to hit the ball? Did the batters hit the ball into space, away from the fielders?

Follow up activity
Many of the practices striking the ball can be done using a cricket-style bat and the game of rota-cricket can be introduced.

CHAPTER 4

Athletics

Running, jumping and throwing are probably the most natural of activities that children engage in during their physical play. These actions provide the foundation for many, if not all, of the physical activities that they may ever be involved in in the future, both in terms of skill and conditioning. Because of the essential nature of these activities they can be seen in many other activity areas but in a different form.

Developing and extending the actions of running, jumping and throwing in a challenging context that encourages vigorous activity and optimum effort is important for each child to develop their full potential and reap the physiological benefits in improved strength, stamina and skill. The activities included here move away from individual races to encourage wider participation, thus changing the emphasis from the best, or the winner, to acknowledging everyone's effort and participation. It is the teacher's responsibility to ensure that every child has ample opportunity for retaining interest and making best progress, developing not only skills, but also positive attitudes.

The activities also aim to emphasise and develop safety awareness and responsibility and provide many opportunities for mathematics in a practical and stimulating context. The mathematical focus will give children the opportunity to talk about measurement and time in a specific but non-threatening way, enabling them to use and assimilate some of the more abstract concepts.

The ancient Olympics

The Greeks took a great interest in athletics and founded the most famous of athletic festivals at Olympia in 776 BC. Every four years, citizens and athletes from all over the Greek world visited Olympia for the festival, held in honour of the god Zeus. (Stories of Zeus from Greek mythology might provide a good background to these lessons.) The games, held at Olympia, (the permanent setting for the event) were a combination of religious worship and athletic competition (a sports stadium like Wembley and a place of religious devotion like Canterbury Cathedral). Athletes came from hundreds of miles away to worship Zeus and to compete in the Games at the grove known as Altis, his most sacred place. Over the years, statues and altars were built to celebrate both athletic and military achievement. Often, the Games lasted from one to three months and a truce from the wars was enforced while the Games took place.

Much of the knowledge we have today of the ancient Olympics has come from archaeological remains, particularly the decorations on pottery.

The ancient Olympics

Using an investigation of the ancient Olympics as the starting point, this series of lessons will encourage children to think about, practise and improve their running (short distance and sustained), jumping and throwing in a different (historical) context.

Four main activities with a historical bias have been selected to form the basis of this unit:
● a *stade* run (short sprint – one length of the stadium)
● a standing jump (without and with using arms)
● a throw (underarm and then linear discus type with quoit)
● a *dolichos* (long-distance foot race)

The lessons will provide excellent opportunities to practise many mathematical activities, including estimating, pacing, measuring and timing.

The unit is divided into six sessions allowing 30–45 minutes of activity per session. Depending on the time available, the activities can be extended or organised in a number of ways as appropriate for your school context. Over a period of several weeks, children will work collaboratively and have more than one opportunity to try each event so that they can see their improvement and be pleased with their progress. They will also be able to compare different ways of doing each activity (for example the standing jump without and then with the assistance of their arms).

Involve children in taking responsibility for taking out, checking and using equipment safely, efficiently and collectively. Mixed-ability groupings will enable children to support each other in the measuring tasks.

Differentiation will be mostly by outcome as individuals or groups are challenged to practise to improve their personal performance. Individuals should be encouraged to beat their own record rather than compare themselves with others.

UNIT: The ancient Olympics

Enquiry questions	Learning objectives	Teaching activities	Learning outcomes
What is the _stade_ run?	● Develop a safety code for athletics. ● Learn how to prepare the body for exercise. ● Prepare for and practise the _stade_ run or short sprint. ● Practise a standing start. ● Introduce and practise a hopping relay.	Warm-up: jogging at different speeds, stretching. Development: hopping on the spot; practising _stade_ run and standing start. Relay: hopping in threes. Cool-down: slow-motion running, playing 'Chinese puzzle'.	Children: ● think about and discuss their sprinting
What is the _dolichos_ run?	● Follow instructions to set out and modify equipment. ● Prepare for and practise the _dolichos_ run (longer run). ● Prepare for and practise throwing for accuracy. ● Further understanding of preparing the body for exercise. ● Introduce and practise a jumping relay.	Warm-up: running lifting their knees and in short bursts; stretching. Development: throwing beanbags for accuracy; running a _dolichos_. Relay: jumping in threes. Cool-down: jogging; playing 'Chinese puzzle'.	● follow instructions and take responsibility for setting out their equipment ● sustain their running ● increase the accuracy of their throws
Can we perform a standing jump?	● Develop understanding of warming up the body. ● Practise the _stade_ run and the standing start. ● Introduce and practise the standing jump. ● Collaborate with a partner to measure and record best performances in the standing jump. ● Introduce and practise a beanbag relay.	Warm-up: jogging at different speeds. Development: practising _stade_ run and standing jump. Relay: running in fours. Cool-down: walking to relax; breathing slowly.	● co-operate well to measure events ● discuss the importance of body preparation for games and the need to warm up even in hot weather
What are the _hoplitodromas_ and the _diaulos_?	● Practise and time the _stade_ run, with and without weights. ● Introduce the _diaulos_ (twice the _stade_). ● Use non-standard measures to measure the running distance. ● Use a stopwatch to time a short run. ● Introduce and practise a throwing relay.	Warm-up: running on the spot; jogging behind one another. Development: running, timing; running with weights. Relay: throwing and running. Cool-down: walking, relaxing, breathing deeply.	● organise, practise, measure and time their running ● record their times clearly
How do our arms help us to jump?	● Practise, measure and compare the standing jump with and without arms. ● Practise steady running for the _dolichos_ run. ● Introduce and practise a hoop relay.	Warm-up: estimating, jogging between beanbags. Development: practising standing jumps; practising _dolichos_. Relay: running, using hoops as obstacles. Cool-down: walking quickly, then slowly.	● understand the importance of the cool-down ● practise and improve the exercises ● understand why there is a difference in the results obtained for the different ways of jumping
Can we beat our running and throwing records?	● Practise a longer run (_dolichos_), increasing the distance covered. ● Practise and measure a throw, trying to beat the record distance. ● Introduce and practise a run-and-jump relay. ● Review progress made.	Warm-up: jogging; leading and following. Development: practising _dolichos_; throwing underarm for accuracy. Relay: running a shuttle relay. Cool-down: walking quickly, then slowly; breathing deeply.	● work well together to improve their personal bests ● record information correctly.

Cross-curricular links
History: examining the ancient Greeks.
Science: investigating the effect of optimum effort on the body.
PSHE: taking fair turns, performing co-operative group activities; keeping safety awareness.
Mathematics: measuring, estimating, timing, recording.
ICT: recording data.

Resources
Cones; beanbags; chalk; hoops; stopwatches; tape measures; metre rules; quoits; photocopiable pages 132–4.

Display
Pictures of the ancient Greeks, with a particular emphasis on the Olympics; an enlarged copy of photocopiable page 134.

The ancient
Olympics

(40 mins) What is the *stade* run?

Learning objectives
● Develop a safety code for athletics.
● Learn how to prepare the body for exercise.
● Prepare for and practise the *stade* run or short sprint.
● Practise a standing start.
● Introduce and practise a hopping relay.

Lesson organisation
Classroom introduction; individual warm-up; practice individually and in threes; relay in threes; cool-down in groups of six; teacher led classroom review.

Vocabulary
stade run
increase
decrease

What you need and preparation

You will need: cones, beanbags or chalk to mark the start and finish of the sprint race; beanbags for markers.

In the classroom, discuss with the children what they know about the present day Olympic Games. *When and how did they begin?* Lead on to a discussion about the ancient Olympics. *What might it have been like to compete in the ancient Olympic Games? What athletic events might the Greeks have participated in? Did women compete? What is special about athletics?* (Optimum effort – fastest, longest, highest.) Discuss the need for competing safely and the special precautions that need to be made for athletics. Ask the children to devise their own safety code (for example looking before they throw or jump; checking before using the space).

What to do

(6 mins) Warm-up

Ask the children to run slowly on the spot, on the balls of their feet, gradually increasing the speed of the action.

Using all the space, ask them to jog slowly in and out of the spaces between everyone else. On the command *Go*, encourage them to increase the pace, and on the command *Slow*, to decrease the pace. Alternate several times. Then add the command *Change*, asking the children to change direction when they hear the word. Encourage good use of space. Vary the commands until the children are breathing heavily. Ask them what they notice about their breathing and pulse rate.

Now tell them to stand tall and to take a big, deep breath and then to stretch each arm above their heads several times in turn and then to circle the hips several times in both directions. Ask them to rock from heels to toes several times and then to repeat one of those exercises.

(14 mins) Development

Ask the children to hop on the spot and then around the playground, getting faster and slower as you instruct. Encourage them to use their arms to help them, and to keep their heads up. Remind them to swap legs occasionally. Then ask them to jog and then run faster and then jog again.

The ancient
Olympics

Ask the children to get into threes and to collect beanbags or chalk. Ask them to prepare and practise for the *stade* run, or short sprint, by deciding on the starting line (use a side of the netball court or similar) and pacing out a finishing line about 30 large strides away (they could estimate this first) and marking these with chalk or beanbags. Ask them to practise short, fast runs in turn between the lines, individually, not racing. Insist that they slow down gradually, and ask them why this is important.

Now let them try out different ways of using their arms as they run (with arms straight or bent; forwards and backwards or across the body). Ask: *Does it make a difference?* Discuss and try out the possibilities, then encourage the children to practise with their arms in opposition to their legs, running at least 20 metres.

Move on to trying different ways of doing a standing start. Ask the children: *Which position will help you with a fast start?* Let them try a few ways and then practise with one foot up to the line. Tell them to try each foot forward in turn. Then let them select which leg they like to lead with (toes up to, but behind the line) and to practise standing starts in their own time.

Ask the children to practise a standing start with one of them shouting *Go* or *Apite* (the Greek word for 'go') for the others to sprint the distance. Change over so they all have a turn at being the starter and several practises of sprinting.

(12 mins) Relay

Introduce a hopping relay in threes. Two children (numbered 1 and 3) stand facing the third child (number 2), ten metres apart. Explain that on *Go*, number 1 hops on one foot towards number 2, and touches the hand of that child. When touched, number 2 hops towards, and then touches the hand of, number 3, who then hops to touch number 1. When number 1 is touched, they switch feet, and the hops are continued until everyone is back in their original place.

(8 mins) Cool-down

Ask the children to practise a slow-motion running action.

Then teach the game 'Chinese puzzle'. Organise the children in groups of six in a circle, taking it in turns for one person to stand to the side (eyes closed) ready to solve the puzzle. The rest of the group hold hands in the circle, and without letting go, try to muddle up their positions. (They can step across or move under their hands.) When they are in a knot they ask the person standing to the side to try to release them, again, without them letting go of each other's hands.

Classroom review

Ask the children which leg they preferred to put forward for their standing start. Ask them to think about their arm action. *What slows you down?* (Unnecessary movement from side to side – flapping.) *What helps?* (Arms bent at right angles, moving in opposition to the legs.)

Assessing learning outcomes

Can the children think about and discuss their sprinting – particularly the arm action?

(40 mins) What is the *dolichos* run?

Learning objectives
● Follow instructions to set out and
modify equipment.
● Prepare for and practise the
dolichos run (longer run).
● Prepare for and practise throwing
for accuracy.
● Further understand preparing the
body for exercise.
● Introduce and practise a jumping
relay.

Lesson organisation
Classroom discussion; individual
and paired warm-up; practise
running individually and in threes;
relay in threes; cool-down in
groups of six; teacher-led classroom
review.

Vocabulary
dolichos run (longer
distance foot race)
starting from scratch
adding and taking
 away points
turning post

What you need and preparation

You will need: beanbags; hoops; stopwatches.

In the classroom, discuss with the children what they know about preparing the body for exercise. The Greeks, it seems, prepared themselves for exercise and competition like modern athletes. Their exercises were described as running on the spot, squats, beating the chest and short, sudden sprints.

What to do

(8 mins) Warm-up

Ask the children to run on the spot, starting slowly and gradually accelerating and decelerating. Encourage them to try with their arms at their sides, and then with their arms moving. Ask: *Is it better to use straight or bent arms?* Encourage them to use bent arms moving in opposition to the legs.

Ask them to practise running, lifting their knees, on the spot and then around the space.

Let them practise running, lifting their heels (to touch their bottoms).

Encourage them to practise running with short bursts of quick, pitter-patter steps.

Now in pairs, ask the children to join hands facing each other. Without letting go, encourage them to raise their arms slowly to one side and above the head (so that they are turning back to back) and down to return to the starting position. Ask them to try it in both directions.

(14 mins) Development

Ask the children to collect two beanbags (or four if available) and a hoop between two, and to place the hoop about ten metres away from a throwing line (a side of the netball court, for example), with as much space as possible between groups.

Encourage them to practise throwing the beanbags into the hoop in as many ways as possible (overarm, underarm, tossing it with two hands underarm or over the head). Remind them to aim and be as accurate as they can. Ask them to throw all the beanbags and then collect them all. If space is limited, do this as a class.

Ask the children to devise a counting system (or suggest starting with five points and add one point for each accurate throw and take away one point for each missed throw). Some pairs may need to be changed to allow a close match of ability for this throwing exercise.

As they practise throwing the beanbags into their target, encourage them to gradually move their hoop further away (two metres at a time) until it is as far as they both can throw. How many times can they hit the target? For safety, ensure that *all* the children throw and then *all* collect.

Encourage as many attempts as time allows, thus allowing plenty of time for practise and improvement. Ask the children to think about ways in which they could improve their actions. Discuss stepping into the throw (with the leg opposite to the throwing arm) and following through at the end of the throw (reaching towards the target). Ask them to pace out the distance thrown to estimate their best mark.

Introduce the *dolichos* (long-distance foot race) by asking each pair to measure out the *stade* distance they used last week (approximately 00 40 metres). Use cones or beanbags as markers. Ask the children how long they think it might take to run there and back twice. Running together, or taking it in turns, ask them to run steadily around both the markers (turning to the left of each marker). Introduce them to them term 'turning gate' or 'turning post' – a marker used for runners to run around in longer races. Ask each pair: *How long does it take?* If there is time, ask them to increase the distance between the posts, seeing if they can still run the distance in the same time.

Relay

Introduce a jumping relay in threes. This is essentially the same as for the hopping relay (see page 93) – the children are numbered 1, 2 and 3, and stand ten metres apart. Instead of hopping, they jump two feet to two feet, backwards and forwards when touched until they are all back in their starting places.

Cool-down

Ask the children to jog slowly in their pairs. On your signal, ask each pair to join another pair and then another to get into groups of six. Remind them how to play 'Chinese puzzle' (see page 93). In a circle, they take it in turns for one person to solve the puzzle by undoing the human knot without separating their hands. The rest of the group hold hands and without letting go, try to muddle up their positions. Make sure the children take turns to solve the puzzle. Then ask them all to shake and relax.

Classroom review

Discuss with the children the conventions of fair turns and good sporting behaviour (for example, the concept of false starts and an equal number of goes). Encourage them to describe what it felt like to run the longer distance. Ask: *What is the difference between a sprint and a steady running action?*

Assessing learning outcomes

Can the children follow instructions and take responsibility for setting out their equipment? How well are they able to sustain their running? How accurate are their throws?

The ancient
Olympics

40 mins Can we perform a standing jump?

Learning objectives
● Develop understanding of warming up the body.
● Practise the *stade* run and the standing start.
● Introduce and practise the standing jump.
● Collaborate with a partner to measure and record best performances in the standing jump.
● Introduce and practise a beanbag relay.

Lesson organisation
Classroom discussion; individual and paired warm-up; paired development; relay in threes; individual cool-down; teacher-led classroom review.

Vocabulary
stade run
starting from scratch
circulating
released

What you need and preparation
You will need: stopwatches; photocopiable page 132; writing materials; beanbags; tape measures.

In the classroom, discuss what it might be like to compete in the height of the summer. *Why do you need to warm up even in hot weather?* Develop this into a discussion on body preparation for athletics.

What to do

6 mins Warm-up
Ask the children to run on the spot, starting slowly and gradually accelerating and decelerating. Encourage them to practise running lifting the knees and then lifting the heels. Practise short bursts of pitter-patter steps.

Ask the children to run fast on the spot for five seconds. Repeat, with a slow jog for ten seconds in between.

In pairs, ask the children to collect two beanbags and to choose a big space in the playground in which to place them, at least 20 metres apart. With the first partner leading, they run to one beanbag, then jog to the other, one behind the other. They continue to run and jog alternately (about three times) until you ask them to change over leaders and repeat the task.

Ask everyone to stand in a space and circle their arms above their heads, backwards and forwards.

16 mins Development
Individually or in pairs, ask the children to practise the *stade* – short, fast runs between two lines. Repeat, asking them to practise their positioning for a standing start, with their chosen foot up to the line.

In twos, ask them to set up and then practise a standing jump, from two feet (toes behind the line) to two feet. Advise them to swing their arms to help them jump (see Diagram 1). Encourage lots of trials and helpful comments.

Ask them to think about fair ways of measuring the jump. *Where will you measure from or to? Will you measure to the heel or the toes, to the front foot or the back foot?*

Diagram 1

Ask them to record their attempts to demonstrate improvement on photocopiable page 132. Ask them to plan how they might modify their own action or that of their partner, or help themselves improve by making simple constructive suggestions, using the back of the photocopiable sheet.

To finish, ask the children to return all equipment to the baskets.

12 mins Relay
Introduce a beanbag relay to the children, in groups of four. Ask each group to collect two hoops and one beanbag per group, and to set out the hoops 20 metres apart. Ask two of

the children to stand behind each hoop facing each other, with the beanbag in one of the hoops. Number the children 1, 2, 3 and 4 and demonstrate the relay using one group. On *Go*, runner 1 picks up the beanbag from the hoop and, running to the left of the hoop, runs to the other hoop and places the beanbag in that hoop. Runner 2 then picks up the beanbag and runs (to the left side of their hoop) and places the beanbag in the other hoop. Runner 3, then Runner 4 do the same, and the run continues until all runners are back in their starting places.

Cool-down
6 mins Ask the children to walk slowly around and then relax, standing in a space. Ask them to breathe slowly in through the nose and then out again slowly. Then ask them to breathe in and hold their breath for the count of three, and then slowly release the air. Help them to imagine the breath rising to the top of their head and then circulating around the body before it is released.

Classroom review
Encourage the children to describe what they have done, and how they might do better, and to record their results in an individual booklet or on a computer spreadsheet.

Assessing learning outcomes
How well did the children co-operate to measure these events? Can they discuss the importance of body preparation for the games and the need to warm up even in hot weather?

40 mins What are the *hoplitodromas* and the *diaulos*?

What you need and preparation
You will need: photocopiable page 133; writing materials; stopwatches; chalk; beanbags; hoops; weights – large balls, small, heavy balls or hand weights.

In the classroom, explain or remind the children how to use a stopwatch. Give some background to the Olympic events. The ancient Greeks used to have a race called the *hoplitodromas* which was a race in armour. Over the years the race was changed and athletes just carried the heavy shield. Ask: *What do you think might happen if you tried to sprint carrying a weight? Would you be faster or slower?* They also had a race called the *diaulos*, which was twice the *stade* (to the turning post and back).

What to do
Warm-up
6 mins Ask the children to run on the spot, starting slowly and gradually accelerating and decelerating. Encourage them to practise running, lifting their knees and then lifting the heels alternately. Practise short bursts of pitter-patter steps.

Let them practise fast running on the spot for five seconds and then ten seconds.

Learning objectives
● Practise and time the *stade* run, with and without weights.
● Introduce the *diaulos* (twice the *stade*).
● Use non-standard measures to measure the running distance.
● Use a stopwatch to time a short run.
● Introduce and practise a throwing relay.

Lesson organisation
Classroom discussion; warm-up and practice individually and in threes; relay in threes; individual cool-down; teacher-led classroom review.

The ancient Olympics

Vocabulary
hoplitodromas
Herakles
diaulos

Organise the children into threes. Ask one of the three to begin leading, alternating jogging with short bursts of speed, while the other partners try to keep up. Change over leaders at regular intervals.

(16 mins) Development

Individually, ask the children to practise short, fast runs between two lines.

Back in threes, ask them to pace out 30 large steps (about 25–30 metres), and to mark a starting line and a finishing line with chalk. Ask them to take it in turns – one starting, one sprinting and one timing. The starter is to shout *Go* or *Apite* for the sprinter to run the distance. Remind them to slow down gradually after crossing the finish line. Change over so that they all have two goes in each role. Take it in turns also to time each runner using a stopwatch or counting to estimate the number of seconds taken to run the distance. Ask them to record their results on photocopiable page 133.

Those who are finding the activity easy can be challenged to lengthen the sprint to 40 or 50 metres. Remind them to practise and use the standing start. Ask them all to measure the distance so that it is the same next time, by using pigeon steps (*Herakles* – using pigeon steps as a non-standard measure).

Ask all the children to try the run again, this time carrying a weight to represent the armour used in the *hoplitodromas*. Prompt their responses by asking: *Can you beat your record? Can you run as fast holding a weight?* Tell them to record their times on photocopiable page 133.

Ask the children to estimate how long it would take to run twice the distance of the *stade* (there and back, round the turning post). *Will it take twice as long?* Let them practise and time the *diaulos* and record their times.

Ask them to measure the distance so that it is the same next time, using the *Herakles* method.

To finish, tell everyone to return their equipment to the baskets.

(12 mins) Relay

Introduce a throw-and-run relay in groups of three or four. Ask each group to collect two hoops and one beanbag, and to set out the hoops 15 metres apart. Ask them all to stand behind one hoop. On your signal *Go*, the first runner stands in the hoop, picks up the beanbag and throws it underarm into the other hoop. They then run to retrieve the beanbag, and run with it back to the starting hoop, placing it there for number two to pick up and throw. The other runners do the same, and the run continues until all runners are back in their starting places. Explain that if the throw is missed, the beanbag should be picked up, but must be touched down in the hoop before the run is continued.

(6 mins) Cool-down

Ask the children to walk slowly into a space, sideways and then backwards. Then instruct them to pause, relax and breathe deeply.

Classroom review

Ask the children to discuss and then record their results. *What difference did the weight make to your running times? Did you take twice as long to run the diaulos as you did to run the stade?*

Assessing learning outcomes

Are the children able to organise, practise, measure and time their running? Are they able to record their times clearly?

(40 mins) How do our arms help us to jump?

What you need and preparation

You will need: photocopiable pages 132 and 134; writing materials; chalk; beanbags; tape measures; metre rules; hoops.

In the classroom, talk about how, in the ancient Olympics, jumpers used to hold weights or *halteres* in their hands to help them jump. Ask: *Do you think you would jump further with weights in your hands?* Explain that instead of using weights, we are going to see if using and not using our arms to jump makes any difference. *Do you think not using your arms might help or hinder you?* Talk them through the diagram on photocopiable page 134.

What to do

(7 mins) Warm-up

Ask the children to jog around the playground, and on *Stop*, to get into threes and to collect six beanbags from the baskets, placing them at least ten metres apart in a large space. Can they estimate ten metres? With one of them leading and the others following, ask them to jog between the beanbags. When they get back to the first one, the second person leads, jogging to beanbags in any order, and then the third.

Ask them to repeat this activity, jogging and then running faster alternately between the cones. Stress no overtaking and ensure they keep changing over leaders.

(18 mins) Development

Now in pairs, ask the children to set up and then practise a standing jump, from two feet (toes behind the line) to two feet. Remind them to swing their arms to help them jump. Encourage lots of trials, adjusting the beanbag or chalk mark if the distance is improved. Tell them to measure the distance jumped with pigeon steps, a tape measure or a metre rule and record their best jumps. Ask: *Can you remember the fair way of measuring the jump?* Advise them to measure from the start line to the heel of the back foot, and record their results on photocopiable page 132.

Ask them to try the standing jump again, but this time without using the arms to help the jump. *Does it make a difference to the jump? How much?* Advise them to record their results on photocopiable page 132 in order to compare the difference.

Ask them to practise, on their own, steady running for the *dolichos* by running backwards and forwards across the playground as many times as they can in one minute (or two minutes).

(12 mins) Relay

Introduce a there-and-back relay with hoops, and children in groups of three or four. Ask each group to collect two hoops and to set them out 15 metres apart. Ask them all to stand behind one hoop. On *Go*, the first runner stands in the hoop, picks it up with two hands and brings it over their head, and places it on the floor again. They then run to the next hoop, and repeat this action before running back to the first hoop, to repeat the action once more before the next runner starts. All the runners do the same in turn, and the run continues until all runners are back in their starting places.

(3 mins) Cool-down

Ask the children to space out and walk quickly, then slowly around the space. Advise them to be aware of how their bodies feel, their breathing and heartbeat.

Learning objectives
- Practise standing jumps, measure and compare with and without arms.
- Practise steady running for the *dolichos* run.
- Introduce and practise a hoop relay.

Lesson organisation
Classroom discussion; individual and paired warm-up; develpment individually and in threes; relay in threes; individual cool-down; teacher-led classroom review.

Vocabulary
halteres
there and back
compare

The ancient
Olympics

Classroom review
Ask the children why the cool-down is so important. Discuss with them gradually bringing the heart and breathing rates back to normal, reducing possible stiffness by taking away lactic acid and calming and settling for other activities.

Assessing learning outcomes
Do the children understand the importance of the cool-down? Are they able to practise and improve the exercises? Do they understand why there is a difference in the results obtained between jumping with and jumping without using their arms?

(40 mins) Can we beat our running and throwing records?

Learning objectives
● Practise a longer run (*dolichos*), increasing the distance.
● Practise and measure a throw, trying to beat the record distance.
● Introduce and practise a run-and-jump relay.
● Review progress made.

Lesson organisation
Classroom discussion; warm-up individually and in threes; individual and in paired development; relay in groups; individual cool-down; teacher-led classroom review.

Vocabulary
dolichos
turning gate
quoit

What you need and preparation
You will need: photocopiable page 133; writing materials; beanbags; hoops; quoits; stopwatches; tape measures.

In the classroom, ask the class to estimate the time they might take to run the *dolichos* if they run four times around the post rather than two. *Will it take double the time? How long do you think six or eight times might take?*

What to do

(8 mins) Warm-up
Ask the children to jog around the space, and whenever you say a number, to get into groups of that number. Finish the exercise with *Three*.

Ask each three to collect six beanbags, and to space them out as they did last time (see page 99). Taking it in turns to lead, ask them to follow the leader as they jog or run more quickly between the beanbags.

(16 mins) Development
Organise the children into pairs and practise the *dolichos* (long distance foot race) by asking each pair to measure out 40 large strides or metres. Use beanbags as markers. Ask them how long they think it might take to run there and back four times. Running together, or taking it in turns, ask them to run steadily around the marker (turning gate) and back around the starting marker four times. *How long does it take?* Ask them to record their results on photocopiable page 133.

Ask them to increase the distance of the longer race by running six to eight times the sprint distance. Count the runs there and back around the cone (the turning gate). Ask them to have two goes with a rest in between, and to record their results on photocopiable page 133.

Ask the children to collect two beanbags (four if available) and a hoop between two and to place the hoop about 20 metres away from a throwing line (for example a side of the netball court). Ask them to practise throwing the beanbag into the hoop using an underarm throw, aiming for accuracy. Challenge them to gradually move it further away until it is as far as they can throw.

Encourage as many attempts as time allows, thus allowing plenty of time for practise and improvement, keeping the furthest beanbag in place to try to beat that distance.

Remind the children about ways in which they could improve their actions (for example follow through, reaching towards the target). Can they measure their longest throw? Ask them to try the same underarm throw for distance using a rubber ring (quoit). Tell them to record their results on photocopiable page 133.

12 **Relay**
mins Introduce a variation of a shuttle relay run in groups of four. Ask each group to split into twos and to stand on lines 20 metres apart, facing each other. Number them from 1 to 4 and demonstrate the relay using one group. On *Go*, runner 1 runs towards the other pair (2 and 4) and around them, crouching down as small as possible in front of them. Runner 2 then jumps over that runner, and runs to and around runner 3, crouching down in a similar manner in front of them. Runner 3 then jumps over runner 2, and the game continues until all runners are back in their starting positions.

4 **Cool-down**
mins Ask the children to walk quickly and then slowly around the space, then to take a deep breath and relax.

Classroom review
Ask the children how they felt as they increased the distance of the steady run. *Did they beat their running and throwing records?*

Assessing learning outcomes
Are the children working well together to improve their personal bests? Are they able to record the information correctly?

Follow-up activities
● Ask the children to write about one or more of the events in the ancient Olympic Games.
● Encourage the class to think about the Olympic motto. *What do the rings represent? Which legends tell the story?*

Outdoor and adventurous activities

There is no one way of teaching outdoor and adventurous activities (OAA). Some schools may take children for an activity week that may incorporate some OAA with residential experience. Other schools may take children for visits to an environmental centre for this part of the PE programme. Much will depend on the local environment and activities provided by local centres. Check BAALPE and LEA safety guidelines with regard to risk assessment before planning.

Many varied activities, however, are possible in the school grounds with relatively little equipment, including those that:

- challenge children physically
- challenge children in a problem-solving capacity
- develop simple orientation and mapping skills
- encourage children to be sensitive to their immediate surroundings and wider environment
- encourage group collaboration and co-operation
- need trust and communication
- help to develop an awareness of safety practices
- involve recording and evaluating.

These activities are often exciting because they take place out of doors or in new environments. It is important that children's taste for adventure and risk is encouraged, but kept within rigid safety parameters. With fewer children making their own way to school or able to follow a route without adults, it is important to provide opportunities in which children can grow in confidence and awareness as they find their way around. It is an important survival and life skill to know about safety in different environments and the need to be careful and take precautions.

Team playing does not automatically help children to work well together, but solving problems may help to foster co-operative attitudes, promote social skills and open lines of communication.

Points of the compass

This unit includes activities that can all be set up in the school playground, but some could equally be part of geography or maths assignments. The games and problem-solving activities will help children to understand more about and use the points of the compass. It is hoped that children will have had some experience of using and making plans and maps. A selection of activity trails is provided on pages 141 and 142.

This unit also incorporates some parachute games for a co-operative climax and cool-down part of each session (details of parachute games are contained on photocopiable pages 135–7. Parachutes are easily stored, moveable, are now more readily available, and can involve whole-body movements using variable energy levels. Just holding the canopy of a parachute can be an exciting and different experience, so this needs to be taken into account if they are being used for the first time.

Gentle activities have been selected to help children calm down at the end of each session. In this context they are used as co-operative activities, with the success of each activity very much depending on everyone working together to manipulate one piece of equipment, taking care of each other and working as a team.

It is essential that you make children fully aware of the boundaries of each activity and encourage them to take responsibility for their actions from the start. Involve them in considering safety for each activity and in making decisions about what to wear.

Allow 45–60 minutes for each of these lessons.

UNIT: Points of the compass

Enquiry questions	Learning objectives	Teaching activities	Learning outcomes
Can we find features on a map?	• Practise moving in different directions. • Practise matching symbols in pairs. • Orientate a map of the playground and identify marked features. • Introduce parachute games.	Warm-up: jogging in and out around the playground, changing directions; playing 'Co-operative hoops'. Development: playing 'Matching pairs' in twos, then repeat trying to beat class record; orientating a map and identifying and marking features on it. Parachute games: spreading out the parachute; playing 'Parachute pass' and 'Making waves'.	Children: • co-operate in a game and with the parachute • find where they are on a map
Can we put together a jigsaw map of the playground?	• Practise moving in different directions, responding to instructions. • Play a jigsaw relay, putting together a map of the playground. • Introduce north and orientate a map of the playground. • Trust a partner to lead them blindfolded around the playground. • Co-operate in using a parachute.	Warm-up: skipping in and out, changing directions; playing 'Co-operative hoops'. Development: playing 'Jigsaw relay'; orientating the map and marking North; taking part in a 'trust walk'. Parachute games: playing 'Fanning' and 'Umbrella'.	• look after and trust their partners • listen to instructions and set up the activities • orientate a map correctly
Can we orientate a map and use points of the compass?	• Use points of the compass, responding to instructions in a game. • Orientate a map of the playground and mark points on the map. • Trust and follow the directions of a partner, learning to give clear instructions. • Co-operate in using a parachute.	Warm-up: jogging to different points of the compass; playing a 'points of the compass' game. Development: orientating a map, trying a variation of 'You are here'; playing 'Treasure hunt'; taking part in a 'trust walk'. Parachute games: playing 'Roundabout' and 'Umbrella'.	• remember and use the points of the compass • lead, and give and follow clear instructions
How can we create an island?	• Familiarise with points of the compass. • Practise using points of the compass in a game, responding to instructions. • Orientate a map of the playground and identify marked features. • Plan and draw an island, marking the coastline and other features. • Co-operate to create an island. • Give directions to a partner. • Co-operate in using a parachute.	Warm-up: jogging around the playground to different points of the compass. Development: trying the 'Treasure island' activity in six groups. Parachute games: practising 'Roundabout' and playing 'Ripples'.	• work together to make their island and to use the chute • use the points of the compass

UNIT: Points of the compass

Enquiry questions	Learning objectives	Teaching activities	Learning outcomes
Can we direct a partner to the treasure?	● Practise using the points of the compass in an individual running challenge. ● Replicate and set out a coastline and other features using a map of an island, co-operating in groups. ● Give directions to a partner and follow the directions of others. ● Co-operate when using a parachute.	Warm-up: jogging to different points of the compass; playing 'Compass run', recording individual times. Development: trying the next part of the 'Treasure island' activity. Parachute games: playing 'Meet your partner' and 'Skydivers'.	● follow directions ● set up equipment and follow a plan ● follow a route given to them verbally
Can we use compass points to find the treasure?	● Work together as a group to set up the compass run and run as a team to beat their group record. ● Mark in the points of the compass on their own map of an island. ● Co-operate to set out a coastline and other features of an island using a map. ● Give directions to a partner and follow the directions of others, using the points of the compass. ● Co-operate and work together using a parachute.	Warm-up: jogging to different points of the compass; timing the compass run. Development: trying the next part of the 'Treasure island' activity, using points of the compass. Parachute games: playing 'Skydivers', 'Mushroom', 'Letting go togothor'.	● work together to beat their group record ● give and follow directions using the points of the compass ● use a map to locate their position.

Cross-curricular links

Geography: investigating scale; using maps; matching recognising symbols; using directions; forms of measurement.
Maths: using standard and non-standard measures; using the points of the compass.
PSHE: interacting, communicating and problem solving in a small group; taking turns to lead and follow.
English: communication; following instructions; devising instructions for others; solving problems.

Resources

One or two parachutes; maps of the school grounds; clipboards; writing and drawing materials; stickers (optional); hoops; stopwatches; blindfolds; beanbags; skittles; cones; ropes; mats; metre rules; tape measures; photocopiable pages 138–44.

Display

A map of the school and its grounds, with compass points marked; a map of the area used for the activities, with compass points marked.

(50 mins) Can we find features on a map?

Learning objectives
- Practise moving in different directions.
- Practise matching symbols in pairs.
- Orientate a map of the playground and identify marked features.
- Introduce parachute games.

Lesson organisation
Brief classroom discussion; individual and whole-class warm-up; paired and whole-class development; whole-class parachute game.

Vocabulary
forwards
sideways
backwards
clockwise
anticlockwise
co-operative
parachute
lifting
lowering
billowing

What you need and preparation
You will need: hoops; stopwatch; copies of photocopiable pages 138–40, cut and laminated for each pair; parachute; small stickers (optional). Copy a map of the school grounds onto different coloured card – sufficient for one each or one between two.

In the classroom, discuss with the children the arrangements for gathering as a group (for example using a list of commands such as *Stop* and *Gather around*).

What to do

(5 mins) Warm-up
Ask the children to jog around the playground in different directions, avoiding everyone else. Encourage them to keep moving, changing directions on the signals *Sideways*, *Forwards* and *Backwards*. Ask them what they need to remember when they are going backwards (to be careful of where they are going).

Play 'Co-operative hoops'. Ask each child to collect a hoop and place it in a space. Ask them to remember where their hoop is in the playground by remembering the colour and what it is near or in line with (for example near the end of the building or the edge of the netball court). Give them some guidelines for this. Ask them to jog in and out of all the hoops without touching them and then to return to their hoop. Continue this activity, but each time take a few hoops away. Children whose hoops have been removed should go to the nearest one so they share the remaining hoops until they are everyone is huddled in the last few hoops. Replace the hoops gradually, a few at a time, and the game continues until they all have a hoop again. Organise the children into pairs ready for the Development section and ask one child from each pair to put away their hoop.

(25 mins) Development
Introduce the children to and play 'Matching pairs'. Have a stopwatch ready to time the game.

Using the cards from photocopiable pages 138–140, ask two children to distribute half the picture symbols randomly around one side of the playground. Ask two other children to distribute the other half of the matching pairs around the opposite side of the playground.

Each pair has a hoop as a home base (these should be spread out in the middle of the playground, making sure that each pair has similar distances to run). Explain that one child from each pair runs to collect one picture and then runs to the other side of the playground to search for the matching card. When found, the matching pair is brought back to the hoop so that their partner can then run to match a pair. When both children are back, ask them to put their hands up and wait for you to check their cards. This continues until all the pairs are matched and checked. Record the time taken by the whole group. The cards can then be returned randomly on the appropriate side of the playground, and the activity can be repeated with the class trying to beat their record.

Go on to introduce the class to 'You are here'. Ask each pair (or individual) to collect a map of the playground. As a class (or in smaller groups), walk around together, pausing to orientate the map and to identify features marked on it, for example the gate, the main entrance or a bench.

Ask the children to point to the position they are standing in ('you are here'). If you have some small stickers, they could place these where you stop and then compare places with another pair on return to the classroom. Ask: *What are you near? Where are you on the map?*

(20 mins) Parachute games

Introduce the parachute, unfolding it and spreading it out on the ground.

Play 'Parachute pass'. With everyone holding on to the edge of the chute with two hands, ask them to pass it gently clockwise and then anticlockwise, all keeping in time.

Play 'Making waves'. With each child holding on to the edge with two hands, ask them to gently lift and lower the chute, making it billow like waves. This takes practice to synchronise. Encourage a whole-body action as their arms are lifted and lowered to and from waist height.

Using a few of the children to demonstrate, show the class how to fold up the parachute.

Classroom review

How many correct pairs of cards did the children get in their hoop? What helped them to remember where their hoop was? Ask them if they have seen or handled a parachute before.

Assessing learning outcomes

Did the children co-operate in the 'Matching pairs' game and when handling the parachute? Could they find where they were on a map?

(45 mins) Can we put together a jigsaw map of the playground?

What you need and preparation

Copy a map of the school grounds onto different coloured card. Cut them into jigsaw shapes and ensure that there are sufficient maps for one each. You will also need: hoops; blindfolds; stopwatch; parachute.

In the classroom, revise last week's lesson, and discuss how to orientate a map.

What to do

(10 mins) Warm-up

Ask the children to skip around the playground, around everyone else. Encourage them to keep moving, changing directions on the signals *Sideways, Forwards* and *Backwards*. Remind them to take care when they are going backwards.

Remind them of and play 'Co-operative hoops'. Ask each child to collect a hoop and place it in a space. Ask them to remember where their hoop is in the playground. Prompt them with: *What helped you to remember last time?* Ask them to jog in and out around the hoops, without touching them, and then to return to their own hoop. Gradually take a few hoops away. Children then share the remaining hoops until they are all huddled in the last few hoops. Replace the hoops gradually as the game continues until they all have a hoop again. When the game is over, ask the children to put away the hoops.

(22 mins) Development

Introduce the class to the game 'Jigsaw relay'. Organise the children in six or eight groups or pairs and distribute the jigsaw pieces of each map to different places in the playground. Each group, running one at a time, takes turns to run to collect one piece of their jigsaw (for example the blue pieces). When they have all their pieces, they place them together to make the map and put their hands up when it is complete.

Time the groups, then, one piece at a time, ask the groups put their pieces back where they found them. Each group then collects and pieces together the next colour map in the same way. Help all the groups to orientate the map and demonstrate the position of north.

Learning objectives
● Practise moving in different directions, responding to instructions.
● Play a jigsaw relay, putting together a map of the playground.
● Introduce north and orientate a map of the playground.
● Trust a partner to lead them blindfolded around the playground.
● Co-operate in using a parachute.

Lesson organisation
Brief revision in the classroom; individual and class warm-up; group and paired activities; whole-class parachute games.

Vocabulary
compass
north
south
east
west
blindfold
trust
lead
follow

**Points of the
compass**

In pairs, introduce the children to the 'trust walk'. One person is blindfolded and the other person leads their blindfolded partner around the playground, taking care not to let them bump into anything or anyone else. They are not allowed to say anything (except in emergencies), but should lead their partner by only touching them lightly under the elbow. Ensure the children take it in turns to do this.

(13 mins) Parachute games

Introduce 'Fanning'. Ask half the class to lie down on the floor with their feet in the centre like the spokes of a wheel. The rest of the class gently waft the chute over those lying down. Tell them to swap roles so everyone has an experience of being fanned.

Now introduce 'Umbrella'. Ask all the children to hold on to the edge of the chute with two hands at floor level. Tell them to lift the chute, reaching to full height, and then let go of it, watching the ripples and billowing shapes as it slowly descends. Ask them to sink slowly downwards as the chute does.

Ask one group to fold up the parachute at the end of the session.

Classroom review

Ask the children: *What does it feel like to be blind? Did you trust your partner? What helped you to trust them?*

Assessing learning outcomes

Are the children able to look after and trust their partners? Do they listen to instructions and set up the activities? Are they able to orientate a map correctly?

(50 mins) Can we orientate a map and use points of the compass?

Learning objectives
● Use points of the compass, responding to instructions in a game.
● Orientate a map of the playground and mark points on the map.
● Trust and follow the directions of a partner, learning to give clear instructions.
● Co-operate in using a parachute.

Lesson organisation
Brief classroom discussion; whole-class warm-up; group and paired activities; whole-class parachute games; teacher-led classroom review.

What you need and preparation

You will need: a map of the school grounds (enough copies for one each); clipboards; writing materials; 'treasure', for example beanbags of different colours or post-it notes with letters on, distributed before the lesson); cones; blindfolds.

In the classroom, explain to the children the points of the compass and the boundaries for the treasure hunt activity.

What to do

(8 mins) Warm-up

Start by explaining to the children which direction north is. Place a cone there and at the other main points of the compass, using as much space as is possible. Ask the class to jog towards north and then say *South* for them to jog back in the direction from which they have come. Keep alternating north and south, sometimes saying *North* twice to encourage careful listening.

Introduce the other two points of the compass and play 'North, south, east and west', changing the instructions as the children get part way to the cones.

(30 mins) Development

Remind the class of 'You are here' (see page 106). From the end of the playground, help the children to orientate the map. In pairs, with one map between two (on a clipboard), ask one of them to orientate their maps and to point to a place on the map (for example a

Points of the
compass

corner of the netball court or an entrance to the building). Their partner takes them to that place and then chooses another place for their partner to go to. Ask the pairs to repeat this.

Introduce and play 'Treasure hunt', in pairs with a map each. Ask the pairs to keep together and to search for the treasure hidden around the playground. Starting from the centre (teacher and clipboards), send them off in different directions to find the treasure. They do not remove the treasure but they return to their clipboard and map to enter where the treasure was found.

Remind the children of the 'trust walk'. One person is blindfolded, the other person leads their blindfolded partner around the playground taking care not to let them bump into anything or anyone else. Advise them that this time, they are not allowed to touch their partner and should direct them only with verbal instructions. Can the blindfolded person guess where they are? Again, ensure the children take fair turns at guiding and being led. Some cones could be added around the playground to make this activity more difficult, but stress how careful the guides need to be.

12 mins **Parachute games**
Introduce 'Roundabout'. Everyone holds on to the edge of the chute with two hands and walks round holding the parachute at waist level. Vary the action – side-step, hop, skip and so on. Repeat, making waves by gently billowing the chute.

Repeat the 'Umbrella' activity from the last session (see page 108).

Ask one group to fold up the parachute.

Classroom review
How many pieces of treasure did the children find? Ask them to compare marks on their map with another pair. *Are the marks in the same places? Which bits of treasure did you find that we did not?*

Assessing learning outcomes
Are the children remembering and using the points of the compass? Are they able to lead, and give and follow clear instructions?

Vocabulary
north
south
east
west
co-operative
parachute
clockwise
anticlockwise
billowing

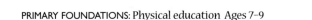

**CHAPTER 5
OUTDOOR
ACTIVITES**

Points of the
compass

(45 mins) How can we create an island?

Learning objectives
- Familiarise with points of the compass.
- Practise using points of the compass in a game, responding to instructions.
- Orientate a map of the playground and identify marked features.
- Plan and draw an island, marking the coastline and other features.
- Co-operate to create an island.
- Give directions to a partner.
- Co-operate when using a parachute.

Lesson organisation
Classroom introduction; whole-class warm-up; group activities; whole-class parachute activities; teacher-led classroom review.

Vocabulary
compass
north
south
east
west
island
coastline
parachute
clockwise
anticlockwise
plan

What you need and preparation
You will need: paper, writing and drawing materials; clipboards; ropes without handles; mats; skittles; cones; beanbags; parachute.

In the classroom, discuss islands with the children. Remind them of the points of the compass, giving them the mnemonic *Never Eat Shredded Wheat* to help them remember. Introduce the 'Treasure island' activity. Tell a story of children who go on a journey in a boat and find an island. They find a map and set out to investigate where treasure is buried.

What to do

(5 mins) Warm-up
Ask the children to jog around the playground together, and pause to face each of the points of the compass in turn.

(30 mins) Development
Explain the 'Treasure island' activity to the class. Remind them of the story you told in the classroom.

In six groups, ask the children to plan the coastline of an island using several ropes to mark out the coastline. Using other equipment like mats, skittles, cones and beanbags, ask the children to arrange features on their island, grouping some and scattering others.

Ensure that they all co-operate to lift and place apparatus and that each child makes a contribution. When complete, ask all the children to make a map by drawing a plan view of their island with its features. Ask them to compare maps with a member of their group, describing the features included. Each child decides where they would want to bury the treasure on the island, and marks the spot with an X, keeping it secret from the others in their group.

Now in pairs, one person puts their map to the side and walks around the island deciding where to land. From that starting point the child with the map directs their partner to their treasure by giving instructions (one step forward, two small steps to the left, one pigeon step

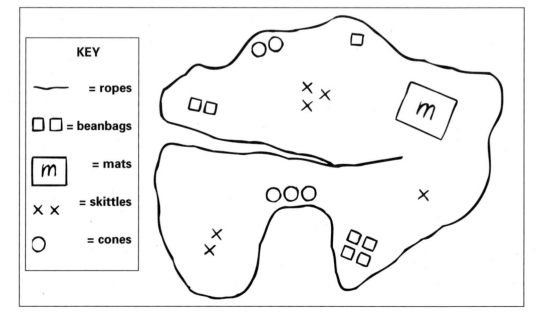

KEY

—— = ropes

□ □ = beanbags

[m] = mats

x x = skittles

○ = cones

110

PRIMARY FOUNDATIONS: Physical education Ages 7–9

backwards, one step up and so on) until they are standing close to the treasure. See how few instructions can be given. Change over with the second person walking around the rope to choose a starting point and their partner using their own map. If there is time, they could repeat this, starting from a different position.

To finish, make sure the group all co-operate to return their apparatus to one side, and that the maps are kept for next week.

10 mins Parachute games

Encourage the children to practise 'Roundabout'. Everyone holds on to the edge of the chute with two hands and walks around, holding the parachute at waist level. Vary the action – side-step, hop, skip and so on.

Introduce 'Ripples'. One after the other, ask the children to lift the edge of the chute and watch the ripples go from one side to the other.

Ask a different group from last time to fold up the parachute.

Classroom review
Discuss with the groups the ways they worked together to create the island. Did they all contribute?

Assessing learning outcomes
Were the children able to work together to make their island and to use the chute? Can they use the points of the compass?

50 mins Can we direct a partner to the treasure?

What you need and preparation
In the classroom, remind the children of the mnemonic *Never Eat Shredded Wheat*, to remember the points of the compass. Look at the 'Treasure island' maps they created last week.

You will also need: writing and drawing materials; equipment used to make the islands (skipping ropes, skittles, mats, beanbags, cones); metre rules; stopwatches; compasses; parachute; copies of photocopiable pages 143 and 144.

What to do

5 mins Warm-up
Starting in the centre of the playground, ask the children to jog to each of the points of the compass in turn, returning to the centre each time, then vary these directions.

33 mins Development
Introduce the game 'Compass run' (taken from the Athletics Ten-step Award). Ask groups of four to collect a metre rule, a stopwatch and five beanbags and to find a big space in the playground as their centre spot (which they mark with a beanbag). Tell them to use the compass (one per group) and line up the pointer at north. Then tell them to measure ten metres north from the centre spot and put down a beanbag as a marker. Similarly, ask them to measure ten metres and mark the spot to the east, south and west. Collect in their compasses.

Learning objectives
● Practise using the points of the compass an individual running challenge.
● Replicate and set out a coastline and other features using a map of an island, co-operating in groups.
● Give directions to a partner and follow the directions of others.
● Co-operate when using a parachute.

Lesson organisation
Brief discussion in the classroom; whole-class warm-up; group and paired activities; whole-class parachute activity; teacher-led classroom review.

Vocabulary
north
south
east
west
skydivers

Points of the compass

Explain the roles of the group members: one starts, one times, one checks the markers are touched and one runs. The runner is timed running from the centre to touch each beanbag with their hand at the four points of the compass, returning to and touching the centre marker each time. Ask the children to record their time on photocopiable page 144. Ensure that they take it in turns and have more than one turn each to try to beat their personal record.

Play 'Treasure island'. Each group is given the maps of their treasure island that were drawn last week. Ask them to exchange these with another group. With this new map, ask each group to decide who is going to put out which piece of apparatus, and then piece by piece they set out the island on the map. Ensure that they all co-operate to lift and place apparatus and that each child makes a contribution.

When complete, ask each child to decide where they would want to bury the treasure on this island and to mark the spot on the map with an X, keeping it secret from the other members of the group. In pairs, one person puts their map to the side and walks around the island, deciding where to land. From that starting point, the child with the map directs their partner to the treasure, by giving simple instructions, until they are standing close to the treasure. Encourage them to see how few instructions need to be given. Tell them to change over, with the second person walking around the rope to choose a starting point and their partner using their own map.

The group then co-operates to put away the apparatus.

12 mins Parachute games

Introduce the game 'Meet your partner'. While the chute is inflated, two children at a time from different sides of the chute can be asked to walk to the centre of the chute to shake hands with their partner before returning to their place to hold on to the edge. All the children could let go of the chute at the same time and freeze in place as they let it fall on them. They could crawl slowly to the edge.

Introduce the game 'Skydivers'. Give children around the chute a number from 1 to 5. Ask all the children to raise and lower the chute. When you call their group number (all the 1s and so on), tell those children to go under the chute and lie down, face up (holding hands) in the form of a star – like skydivers . The remaining players shake the chute up and down on them for a minute or so, until you call that number again and they return to their places and another group number is called.

Ask a group that hasn't done so before to fold up the chute.

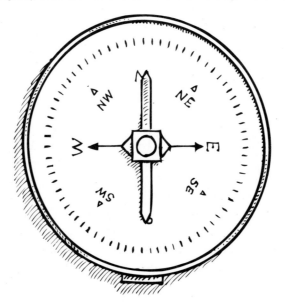

Classroom review

Could the children follow the map to plan the island? What helped them to put the features in the right places? Ask the children to get back into their pairs, and to say one thing that they appreciated about their partner and their contribution to the group effort. For example, *I liked the way you listened, I liked the way that you waited for…* or *I liked your idea of…*

Assessing learning outcomes

Can the children follow directions? Can they set up equipment and follow a plan? Can they follow a route given to them verbally?

55 mins Can we use compass points to find the treasure?

What you need and preparation

You will need: metre rules; stopwatches; beanbags compasses; photocopiable pages 143 and 144; apparatus to create islands (see page 111); parachute.

In the classroom discuss briefly with the children how to play 'Compass run'.

What to do

15 mins Warm-up

As a group, encourage the children to jog to different points of the compass in turn.

Set up the 'Compass run' by asking groups of four to collect a metre rule, a stopwatch and five beanbags and to find a big space in the playground as their centre spot. Using the compass (one in each group if possible), ask them to line up the pointer at north. From the centre spot, tell them to measure ten metres north and put down a beanbag as a marker, and similarly, measure ten metres and mark the spots to the east, south and west. Then take in their compasses.

As a team, ask them to plan how to run this as a relay, and time how long it takes for them to complete the task (starting, timing, checking the markers and each person running in turn). Each child runs from the centre to touch with their hand each of the beanbags at the four points of the compass, returning to and touching the centre marker each time. When they have touched the four points of the compass, they must touch the next runner, who starts from the centre. Record the time it takes the whole group to complete this relay on photocopiable page 144, and encourage them to try again, aiming to beat their record.

25 mins Development

With their own plans of their treasure island that were drawn last week, ask each child to mark in the points of the compass. As a group, ask them to plan and set out their island, doing different jobs this time if possible. Ask them to arrange features on their island, grouping some and scattering others. Check that they all co-operate to lift and position apparatus and that each child makes a contribution. Each child decides where they would want to bury the treasure on the island and marks the spot on the map with an X, keeping it secret from the other members of the group.

In different pairs from those in the previous lesson, one person puts their map to the side and walks around the island, deciding where to land. From that starting point, the child with the

Learning objectives
● Work together as a group to set up the compass run and run as a team to beat their group record.
● Mark in the points of the compass on their own map of an island.
● Co-operate to set out a coastline and other features of an island using a map.
● Give directions to a partner and follow the directions of others, using the points of the compass.
● Co-operate and work together using a parachute.

Lesson organisation
Brief classroom discussion; group warm-up; group and paired activities; whole-class parachute activities; teacher-led classroom review.

Vocabulary
north
south
east
west
taut

map directs their partner to the treasure by giving simple instructions, using points of the compass (one step to the south, two small steps west and so on) until they are standing close to the treasure. Challenge them to see how few instructions need to be given. Change over with the second person walking around the rope to choose a starting point and their partner using their own map.

Now make sure the group all co-operate to put their apparatus to the side. They then exchange maps with another group. As a group, they decide who is going to put out which pieces of apparatus and then try to set out the island on the map. Repeat the exercise, taking it in turns to give a partner instructions to get to the treasure which is marked on their map.

15 mins Parachute games
Remind the class how to play 'Skydivers'. Give the children, around the chute, a number from 1 to 5. Ask everyone to raise and lower the chute. Then, call a group number, for example *Number 1s*, for those children to go under the chute, lie down face up, holding hands, in the form of a star – like skydivers. The remaining players shake the chute up and down on them for a minute or so, until you call that group number again and the children under the chute return to their places. Continue by calling another group number.

Introduce the game 'Mushroom'. Ask the children to start in a crouch position, with everyone holding the edge of the chute with two hands. Gradually rise up onto toes, lifting the edge of the chute until it is held above the head with everyone in a full body stretch. Ask them to hold onto the parachute, placing it behind them as they sit down. Everyone will be sitting inside the dome created.

Ask the children to stand up, to try 'letting go together'. Ask everyone to pull with two hands on the edge of the chute (so it is taut), while it is on the floor. On your *Go* signal, ask them to let go and watch it spring towards the centre.

Classroom review

With a different partner from the review last week, ask the children to say one thing that they have appreciated about their partner, and their contribution to the group effort (for example *I liked the way that you listened, I liked the way that you waited for… It was thoughtful of you to… I liked your idea of…*).

Assessing learning outcomes

Did the children work together to beat their group record? Can they give and follow directions using the points of the compass? Can they use a map to locate their position?

Swimming

Swimming is an essential life skill that all children should have the opportunity to experience whilst at primary school. Where possible, a class should have the continuity of a year's tuition in order to make each child a competent and proficient swimmer. This will vary from school to school, depending upon facilities available, authority guidelines, staffing and expertise available, previous experience of the children, timetabling, transport, funds, and many other factors.

Although the National Curriculum stipulates that all children in this age group should 'be taught to swim unaided for a sustained period of time over a distance of at least 25 metres', ideally to meet the requirements of water-based activities, children should be encouraged to achieve a minimum of 50 metres and be able to swim on their front and back. Basic personal survival skills should be covered, such as treading water, the carrying of equipment, floating and sculling. Each school will need to decide how the swimming National Curriculum requirements are met, but it is important that avenues are opened for water skills learned at school to be continued through social and recreational situations, so that swimming can become a life-long activity.

Those teachers who have to teach swimming without an instructor present at the pool are advised to gain an appropriate swimming qualification. In many LEAs, instruction is provided as part of the service and those instructors should have their own lesson plans for teaching the swimming National Curriculum.

Before the class go swimming it is important that:

● any children suffering from an injury or having any physical disability should be brought to the notice of the swimming instructor. Written notification will help to ensure that appropriate measures are in place on the poolside to cover any emergencies (for example, asthma pumps for asthmatics and a supply of sugar, such as a chocolate bar, for diabetics)

● children should understand the principals of hygiene and develop a habit of using the toilet before entering the water and cleaning themselves under a shower if necessary

● you (or the swimming teacher) are satisfied that the changing areas for both sexes are supervised, especially if shared with the general public

● you should be present at the poolside whilst any of the children are in the water and where possible co-operate with the instructor in the use of group methods of teaching

● lifeguards are present during all schools' swimming in public baths and you are aware where they are situated in case they are required

● emergency equipment should be readily available on the poolside to cover any accident; both the teachers and the lifeguards should be aware of the extent of children's previous swimming experience

● you are aware of any LEA rules or guidance on this strand of PE

● you are aware of any rules associated with health and safety, such as the swimming pool's Code of Behaviour.

For many schools it is a requirement to have an inclusive policy on integration. It is important that any children in this category are catered for at the swimming pool. This might include access ramps for wheelchairs, pool hoists, appropriate changing facilities, correct swimming and buoyancy aids and adequate adult supervision in the water.

In some cases, for cultural or religious reasons, children might be allowed in clothing other than usual swimwear. In such cases, alternative clothing should allow freedom of movement and not seriously affect the child's flotation.

Front and back crawl

This unit focuses on the teaching of front and back crawl for a small, middle-ability group, taken by the teacher under the auspices of a pool or authority swimming instructor. Where swimming instructors are present they will have a half-term or termly plan of work that will include a variety of warm-ups, stroke work (including the use of aids) and some structure-free activity. It is likely that the children in this 'middle' group have recently learned to swim and are now being helped to improve these two strokes and their personal survival skills.

Children should be told where to sit on the edge of the pool, and encouraged to get in by turning on their tummies and sliding gently into the water. Children who are more proficient and competent swimmers will be in the deeper water. The instructor will advise those children who need armbands or any other buoyancy aids. Floats will be required to assist the children to swim. Some time must be allocated to play games that increase water confidence, for example blowing a table tennis ball, collecting objects from the floor of the pool and playing with a ball in the water.

The sample lessons are designed for you to support a middle-ability group working for 25–30 minutes in the shallower water of a large pool.

UNIT: Front and back crawl

Enquiry questions	Learning objectives	Teaching activities	Learning outcomes
What is the correct breathing technique for front crawl?	● Practise continuous swimming freestyle. ● Learn and practise front crawl breathing. ● Practise floating, particularly start floats. ● Introduce surface dives.	Warm-up: practising choice of stroke. Development: practising push and glide, streamlined position and leg kick; practising breathing action to both sides. Cool-down: practising surface dives through hoops, trying head first.	Children: ● breathe correctly after every three pulls ● pike at the hips to dive to go through hoops (using the surface dive entry)
What is the correct arm action for front crawl?	● Practise and improve front crawl arm action. ● Practise front crawl breathing and leg kick. ● Practise whole front crawl stroke. ● Try and practise surface dives, feet first.	Warm-up: practising choice of stroke. Development: practising arm action, breathing and leg kick. Cool-down: practising surface dives through hoops, trying feet first.	● swim front crawl with the correct arm action
What is the correct leg action for front crawl?	● Practise a chosen stroke, with or without a float. ● Practise and improve front crawl leg action. ● Practise the whole front crawl stroke. ● Develop surface diving techniques, collecting objects from the bottom of the pool.	Warm-up: practising choice of stroke. Development: practising front crawl leg kick, practising with faces in the water; practising full front crawl action, emphasising leg action. Group activity: practising front crawl continuous relay. Cool-down: practising head-first and feet-first surface dives.	● movie their legs from the hips in the front crawl ● use both forms of surface dive ● pick up an object from the bottom of the pool with the correct technique
What is the correct leg action for back crawl?	● Learn and practise back crawl leg action. ● Practise jumping into the pool. ● Practise different shapes in the air before entering the water. ● Practise chosen stroke without a float.	Warm-up: practising front crawl without floats. Development: practising the back crawl leg kick and correct body position; practising leg kick and arm action with one arm; trying full back stroke. Cool-down: jumping into the pool making different shapes.	● are able to keep the correct body shape whilst on their backs ● can swim with the correct back crawl leg action
What is the correct arm action for back crawl?	● Introduce and practise back crawl arm action. ● Practise a variety of floating positions. ● Practise and improve chosen stroke.	Warm-up: practising front crawl. Development: practising back crawl leg action and body position; improving back crawl arm action. Cool-down: practising floating in different shapes.	● feel comfortable when swimming back crawl
What is the correct body position for back crawl?	● Practise and improve the body position for back crawl. ● Practise the leg and arm actions for back crawl. ● Practise a variety of floating positions.	Warm-up: practising back crawl. Development: practising back crawl using legs only; practising arm action; practising full back stroke. Group activity: back crawl relay in groups of three. Cool-down: practising floating in different shapes on front and back.	● can float for a considerable time ● improve their back crawl technique.

Cross-curricular links
Science: looking at forces.
PSHE: appreciating the value of swimming as a healthy activity.
English: evaluating and describing swimming activities.

Resources
Floats; armbands; weighted hoops; weighted objects (for life-saving practice).

**Front and back
crawl**

(25 mins) What is the correct breathing technique for front crawl?

What you need and preparation

You will need: floats; armbands; weighted hoops.

In the classroom, discuss swimming safety procedures with the children. Find out how much experience individuals have of swimming, in order to place them in ability groups. Ensure that all the children know where to sit on the poolside when they have changed.

What to do

(5 mins) Warm-up

Ask the children to enter the pool by sliding on their tummies into the water. Holding on to the side, ask them to jump up and down, getting their shoulders under the water. Encourage them to get their faces wet.

Ask them to swim for several minutes, using a choice of stroke. Some children may feel more confident using a float at this stage, but it will be an opportunity to observe them all, checking that they are in the right ability group.

(15 mins) Development

Ask the children to take a few paces back from the side of the pool and to stand with their shoulders under the water and their feet one foot in front of the other, ready to push and glide to the side. Encourage them to take a deep breath and to lie face down on the water, so that the water surface is touching their forehead. Practise the push and glide to the side several times, encouraging a long, streamlined position.

Holding on to the side, ask the children to practise the front crawl leg kick, moving their legs up and down, kicking from the hips. If they can, encourage them to hold their breath and then breathe out under the water.

With a float each, ask them to practise the leg kick action, holding on to the float with two hands, swimming across the width of the pool.

Tell everyone to hold the float out in front of them in their right hand and keep their left arm alongside the rest of the body, lying on their tummy, with the float out in front of them. Encourage them to swim forward using the front crawl leg kick only, and to turn their head to take a breath on the left side of the body, where the arm is beside the body. Make sure that when they are breathing that one ear is left in the water, *turning* their heads rather than lifting them out of the water.

Repeat the activity, asking the children to breathe on the right-hand side and hold their float in their left hand, with the right arm held alongside the body.

Then, using a full front crawl action, ask the children to breathe after every three arm pulls.

Diagram 1

(5 mins) Cool-down

With weighted hoops at various depths of the pool, ask the children to swim through as many as they can. (For hoops that lie half under the water, encourage a streamlined body position, and for those positioned deeper, encourage surface dives, head first – see Diagram 1.)

Front and back
crawl

Encourage the children to swim and take a breath before diving, pulling with both arms, tucking in their head and piking at the hips. Their legs should be lifted into a vertical position for the dive in one continuous movement.

Classroom review
Encourage the children to describe what they were good at and what they enjoyed. Ask them what they had to do in order to go through the hoop without touching it. Discuss the purposes of the surface dive – to submerge quickly to avoid danger.

Assessing learning outcomes
Were all the children breathing correctly after every three pulls? Are they piking at the hips to dive to go through the hoops (using the surface dive entry)?

30 mins What is the correct arm action for front crawl?

What you need and preparation
In the classroom, discuss with the children where they are to sit and the key points of the previous lesson (including breathing after every three arm pulls).

Ensure that floats, armbands and weighted hoops are all accessible to the children.

What to do

5 mins Warm-up
Ask the children to enter the pool by sliding in on their tummies. Ask them to swim four widths of the pool using a choice of stroke.

15 mins Development
Ask the children to lie on their tummies and to hold a float in two hands, to practise kicking with their legs, keeping them long and moving them from the hips. Encourage them to try to keep the rhythm going, emphasising a fast, shallow kick.

Ask the children to hold their float in their left hand, stretched out in front of them. Using the front crawl kick, ask them to pull with their right hand, keeping the arm moving. (See Diagram 2.) Repeat, changing the hand holding the float after every width.

Emphasise big arm pulls with the hands entering the water thumbs first. Encourage a bent-arm recovery (elbow leading) and breathing in when the arm is just completing the pulling action, breathing out when the face is in the water.

Ask the children to perform the whole stroke without a float, encouraging a continuous action (see Diagram 3).

5 mins Free stroke practice
Ask the children to take a few minutes for some free practise, choosing one of the strokes and practising with or without a float.

Learning objectives
● Practise and improve front crawl arm action.
● Practise front crawl breathing and leg kick.
● Practise whole front crawl stroke.
● Try and practise surface dives, feet first.

Lesson organisation
Classroom discussion; whole-class warm-up and activities; teacher-led classroom review.

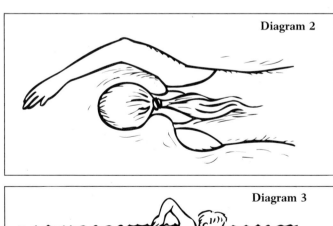

Diagram 2

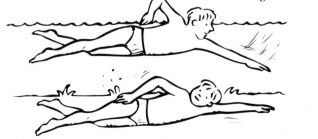

Diagram 3

Front and back crawl

Vocabulary
front crawl
floating
sculling
breathing

⑤ mins Cool-down
As last week, with some weighted hoops at various depths in the pool, ask the children to swim through as many hoops as they can. This time, ask them to try surface dives feet first (see Diagram 4). Encourage them to tread water while they take a deep breath, before kicking and pushing downwards, placing both arms against their sides and bringing their legs together.

Classroom review
Ask the children which arm they found easier to swim with when using a float.

Assessing learning outcomes
Are all the children able to swim front crawl with the correct arm action? What key points need to be covered for the next lesson (arm action, breathing)?

Diagram 4

㉚ mins What is the correct leg action for front crawl?

Learning objectives
● Practise a chosen stroke, with or without a float.
● Practise and improve front crawl leg action.
● Practise the whole front crawl stroke.
● Develop surface diving techniques, collecting objects from the bottom of the pool.

Lesson organisation
Classroom discussion; individual warm-up; whole-class development; small-group activity; individual cool-down; teacher-led classroom review.

What you need and preparation
You will need: floats; armbands; weighted objects.

In the classroom, discuss with the children the work performed over the past sessions, and reinforce swimming pool safety issues.

What to do
⑤ mins Warm-up
Ask the group to practise their chosen stroke, with or without floats.

⑮ mins Development
Ask the children to lie on their tummies and to hold a float with both hands, with arms outstretched, to practise the front crawl leg kick. Encourage the children to have straight legs with pointed toes and loose ankles. Emphasise keeping their legs long and moving them from the hips. Encourage them to keep the rhythm going, using a fast, shallow kick. Tell the children to keep their heads to one side, with one ear in the water at all times (rather than lifting their heads).

Repeat this practice, encouraging the children to keep their faces in the water. Encourage them to blow out into the water before turning sideways to breathe in. If they can, encourage them to try breathing to both sides.

Let everyone practise full front crawl, with emphasis on a fast, shallow leg kick.

⑤ mins Group activity
In groups of four, ask the children to label themselves 'A', 'B', 'C' and 'D'. Using the width of the pool, ask the 'A's and the 'C's to sit on one side of the pool, with the 'B's and D's at the opposite side. Explain that 'A' swims to 'B' using front crawl and breathing after every three pulls. When 'A' has reached the other side, 'B' then swims to 'C', who then swims to 'D', who swims to 'A'. Ask the children to continue like this until all the swimmers reach the side they started from.

Vocabulary
front crawl
floating
breathing

5 mins Cool-down
Place weighted objects around the bottom of the pool and ask the children to retrieve them. The objects should be placed at different depths so that all the children are successful and are being stretched to their potential. Encourage the use of both the head-first and the feet-first surface dives.

Classroom review
Discuss with the children why you are encouraging them to breathe to both sides. Ask them how many weighted objects they retrieved. What is the quickest way to pick up an object from the bottom of the pool? (Swim towards it under the water or surface dive towards it in a straight line.)

Assessing learning outcomes
Are the children moving their legs from the hips in the front crawl? Are they using both forms of surface dive? Are they able to pick up an object from the bottom of the pool with the correct technique?

30 mins What is the correct leg action for back crawl?

What you need and preparation
You will need: floats; armbands.
In the classroom, discuss the work performed over previous sessions.

What to do
5 mins Warm-up
Ask the children to enter the pool by sliding in on their tummies, and to practise the front crawl without floats.

15 mins Development
Ask the group to hold a float with both hands across their chest (or hold it behind their heads like a pillow) and to lie back in the water to practise the back crawl leg kick. Encourage them to stretch their toes and keep their ankles loose, maintaining a continuous flutter action. Like the front crawl leg action, encourage the children to move their legs from the hips rather than bending them at the knees (see Diagram 5).

Ask them to try this without floats, lying on their backs with their arms by their side. In that floating position, encourage the children to kick their legs to propel themselves backwards. Encourage all the children to push their tummy up and look at the ceiling to keep the correct body shape. As they swim across the pool on their backs, all the children should be aware where the wall is that they are swimming towards.

Repeat this, but this time ask the children to hold one float across their chest, using the other arm to swim. The arm entering the water should be straight, with the little finger touching the water first, palm out, and the arm close to the ear.

Ask the children to perform a full back crawl with slow, long arms and fast, straight legs.

5 mins Free stroke practice
Ask the children to spend five minutes practising their chosen stroke.

Learning objectives
● Learn and practise back crawl leg action.
● Practise jumping into the pool.
● Practise different shapes in the air before entering the water.
● Practise chosen stroke without a float.

Lesson organisation
Classroom discussion; individual warm-up; whole-class development and cool-down teacher-led classroom review.

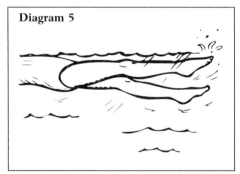
Diagram 5

Vocabulary
front crawl
back crawl
floating
breathing

Front and back
crawl

 Cool-down

Tell the children to try jumping into the pool. Ask them to try various ways: *Can you make a pencil shape? Can you keep their arms stretched above their heads? Can you make a shape in the air before entering, with your feet together? Can you do star jumps?* Remind them to look before they jump. If they have not had previous experience of jumping into the pool, they can be encouraged to bunny jump sideways into the pool, with both hands flat on the side.

Classroom review

Ask the children why they need to push their tummies towards the ceiling whilst practising the back crawl. Ask them why they must kick fast with their legs when swimming the back crawl.

Assessing learning outcomes

Are all the children able to keep the correct body shape whilst on their backs? Do they swim with the correct back crawl leg action?

What is the correct arm action for back crawl?

Learning objectives
● Introduce and practise back crawl arm action.
● Practise a variety of floating positions.
● Practise and improve chosen stroke.

Lesson organisation
Classroom revision; whole-class and individual activities; teacher-led classroom review.

What you need and preparation

You will need: floats; armbands.

In the classroom, revise keypoints raised during the previous lesson.

What to do

 Warm-up

Ask the children to enter the water by sliding in on their tummies, and to practise front crawl, concentrating on big arm pulls.

Development

Lying on their back, ask each child to hold a float across their chest and swim using a back crawl action with the free arm. Stress that the swimming arm must be big and straight at all times, with the little finger entering the water first.

Repeat this, but after one width, tell the children to change the arm that holds the float.

Ask the children to perform a full back crawl action, concentrating on straight arms, with no splashing when their hands enter the water.

 Free stroke practice

Ask the children to spend five minutes practising and trying to improve their chosen stroke.

 Cool-down

Ask the children to lie back in the water to float. Can they make different shapes as they float? Can they try a star shape? Can they count as they do this?

Classroom review

Ask the children how comfortable they felt swimming the back crawl. Ask: *What must you remember to do when swimming the back crawl?* (Look where they are going.)

Vocabulary
front crawl
back crawl
floating
breathing

Assessing learning outcomes

Are all the children successful in swimming the back crawl? What aspects of the back crawl technique do some of the children have to concentrate on?

30 mins What is the correct body position for back crawl?

What you need and preparation
You will need: floats; armbands.

In the classroom, discuss with the children the importance of correct body line in the water when swimming the back crawl.

What to do

5 mins Warm-up
Ask the children to enter the pool by sliding on their tummies, and to practise the back crawl with or without floats.

15 mins Development
Lying on their back with arms by their sides, ask the children to swim across the pool with and then without a float, using only their legs. Encourage them to look at the ceiling and push their tummies up. Remind them to breathe regularly.

Then ask each child to hold a float across their chest and swim using a back crawl action with the free arm. Tell them that the swimming arm must be big and straight at all times, with the little finger entering the water first. Practise this with the other arm.

Tell the children to practise the full back crawl action, remembering:

● the arm action
● the leg action
● the body position (see Diagram 6)
● the correct breathing technique.

Diagram 6

5 mins Group activity
Ask the children to get into groups of three and label themselves 'A', 'B' and 'C', for a back crawl relay. Two children ('A' and 'C') stand in the water on one side of the pool, with the remaining child ('B') on the other side of the width. Explain that 'A' then swims the back crawl to 'B', who stops them before they touch the side, and then swims to 'C'. Continue as a race for four minutes. Ask: *How many times did you go backwards and forwards?*

5 mins Cool-down
Ask the children to lie back in the water to float. Ask them: *Can you make different shapes as you float? Can you try a star shape on your front as well as your back?* Encourage them to put their faces in the water when they float on their front. How long can they stay in each floating position?

Classroom review
Ask the children how long they floated for in their star shapes. Ask them how successful they were in swimming on their backs and why?.

Assessing learning outcomes
Are all the children able to float for a considerable time? Do any practices need to be worked on by some children to achieve the correct back crawl technique?

Learning objectives
● Practise and improve the body position for back crawl.
● Practise the leg and arm actions for back crawl.
● Practise a variety of floating positions.

Lesson organisation
Classroom discussion; individual warm-up; whole-class development; small-group activities; teacher-led classroom review.

Vocabulary
front crawl
back crawl
floating
breathing technique

Lifting feet high apparatus plan

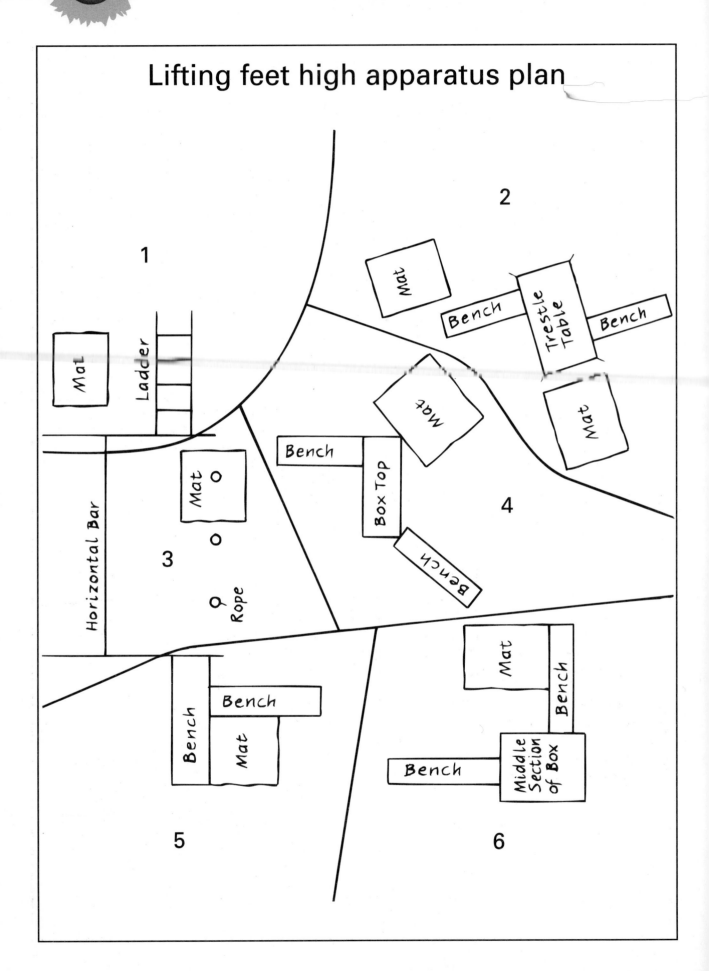

Linking actions apparatus plan

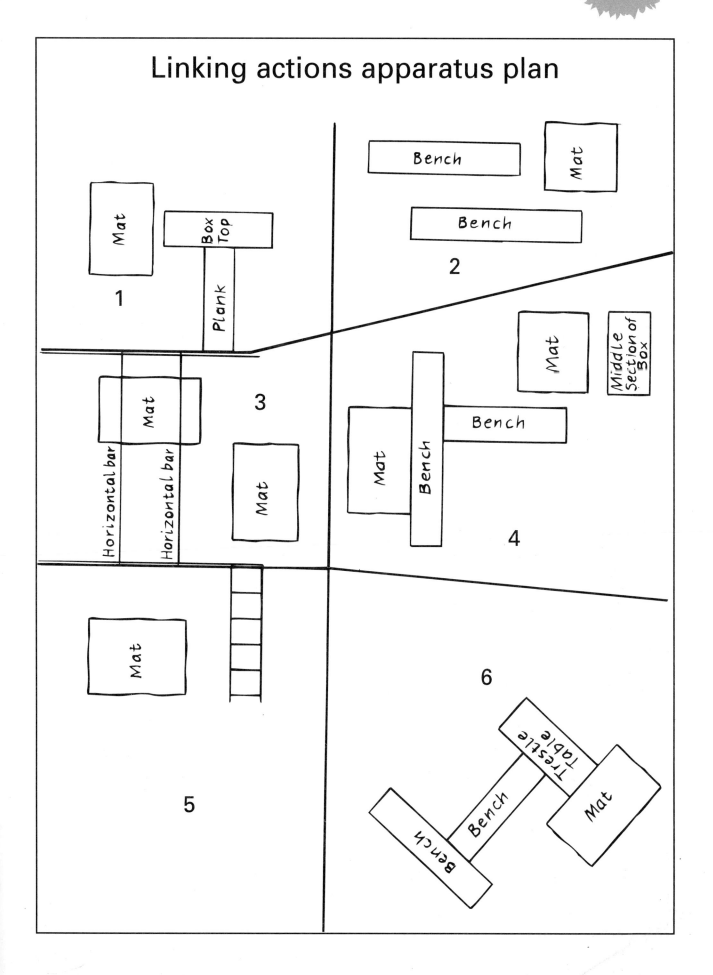

Port and starboard

The children move around the space, without touching one another. Then give out instructions for them to perform:

- **Port** – go to the left.

- **Starboard** – go to the right.

- **Overboard** – lie down on the floor.

- **Row the boat** – sit on the floor and pretend to row a boat.

- **Captain's coming** – stand to attention and salute.

- **Climb the rigging** – find a space and pretend to climb a ladder as fast as you can.

- **Sweep the decks** – walk around the space, pretending to sweep the floor.

- **Scrub the decks** – kneel on the floor and pretend to scrub it clean.

Make up any other appropriate actions as you see fit.

Warm-up games (1)

The bean game

Ask the children to run around the space. When you call out the name of a bean, the class make a shape or perform an action as follows:

- **Runner bean** – run around the space without touching one another.
- **Frozen bean** – immediately stop and stands still.
- **Kidney bean** – lie on the floor on your side, with your knees tucked up to your chest.
- **Baked bean** – lie on your back or tummy in a wide shape.
- **French bean** – walk around in a long, thin shape.
- **Chilli bean** – stand with your arms crossed, pretending to shiver.
- **Jumping bean** – jump around the space, with both feet together.

Points of the compass

The children are shown, in the hall or playground, where the points of the compass are situated.

As they move about the space (walking, running or jogging), call out a compass point, and the children have to run to the corresponding side of the playing area.

Stuck in the mud

This is a whole-class game, starting with one or two of the children nominated as chasers.

The children have to run around the space, trying to avoid being caught by the chasers. When a chaser touches someone, that person has to stand still with their arms out wide (they become 'stuck in the mud'). They can only be released when someone goes under their arms.

The game can get progressively harder by the introduction of more chasers and more complex actions, for example when someone is 'stuck in the mud', they can only be released when someone crawls through their legs.

It is important that the children work co-operatively to support one another when they have been touched.

Warm-up games (2)

Traffic lights

The children move around the space, and when you shout out a colour, they have to perform a corresponding action:

● **Red** – stand still.
● **Amber** – hop around the space.
● **Green** – walk or run around the space.

Alphabet

The children can work as a whole class for this activity, or in small groups.

The children walk around the space, and when you call out a letter of the alphabet, the class or group has to make the shape of that letter within a given time, by lying on the floor.

Numbers

This is basically the same as for the alphabet game above, but instead of letters, you call out a number for the children to make the shape of by lying on the floor within a given time.

Video

The children move about the space, and on your command, perform a corresponding action:

● **Stop** – stay still.
● **Pause** – jog on the spot.
● **Play** – jog around steadily.
● **Fast forward** – jog faster.
● **Rewind** – jog slowly backwards.

Warm-up games (3)

Back to front
In pairs, ask the children to number themselves 1 and 2. Number 1 leads and number 2 follows, jogging about the space.

On your command *Back to front*, the person following sprints in front of their partner and becomes the leader, slowing to jogging, and leading their partner in and out of the spaces, away from other pairs.

Side to side
This is a game involving sudden changes of direction while keeping up with a partner.

In pairs, ask the partners to face each other in a big space, and to label themselves 'A' and 'B'. 'A' moves from side to side, and keeps changing direction after a few steps (sometimes one or two, sometimes three or four), suddenly stopping and starting, but not running away. 'B' shadows their partner, trying to keep up with them and not letting them get more than two strides away.

If, when the whistle blows, 'B' is close to their partner, they score a point. If 'A' is more than two strides away, then 'A' gets a point. Ensure that the children keep changing roles.

Cool-down activities (1)

Deep breathing

The whole class should be relaxed, standing still in a space. Encourage all the children to take a large, deep breath in through the nose, hold it for the count of three, and then slowly release it through the mouth. While they are doing this, encourage them to imagine their breath infusing from the top of their head and then circulating around the whole body before it is released.

Sleeping lions

The children lie down on the floor, keeping very still. If they move, ask them to go and get changed or line up ready to go back to the classroom.

Relaxation

Lying down in a space, ask the children to tense and then relax the whole body, letting it go limp and floppy. Do this a couple of times, then tell them to relax different parts of the body in turn. Vary the action, and finish with the whole body relaxing.

An alternative is for you to select one part of the body to start with, going through all parts in turn until every part is tensed. Encourage the children to hold the whole body tight for ten seconds and then to relax.

Cool-down activities (2)

Chinese puzzle

With the children in groups of four to six, ask the groups to form a circle, with one person standing to the side with their eyes closed.

The rest of the group holds hands in the circle and, without letting go, they try to muddle up their positions (they can step across or move under their hands and so on). When they are in a knot, ask the person who is standing to the side to try to release them again, without separating their hands. Ensure as many children as possible have a go at solving the puzzle.

Circle squeeze

The whole class stands in a circle with you, holding hands. Make up a message of squeezes (for example three short squeezes and two long) and pass it on to the child on your left.

The message is then passed right the way around the circle back to you. Tell the class if it is the same message as you sent at the start.

Slow-motion jogging

Ask the children to move around the space with a jogging action, but as slowly as possible and with clear, exaggerated movements.

Shadowing

In pairs, one partner moves with a particular slow-motion action, and the other follows, copying the action. After 30 seconds, tell the children to change over.

Name _____

Standing jump record card

Distance recorded

Without using arms			Using arms			Furthest jump

ATHLETICS: **The ancient Olympics**

What are the *hoplitodromas* and the *diaulos*? Page 97 and Can we beat our running and throwing records? Page 100   PHOTOCOPIABLE

Name _____

How fast? How far?

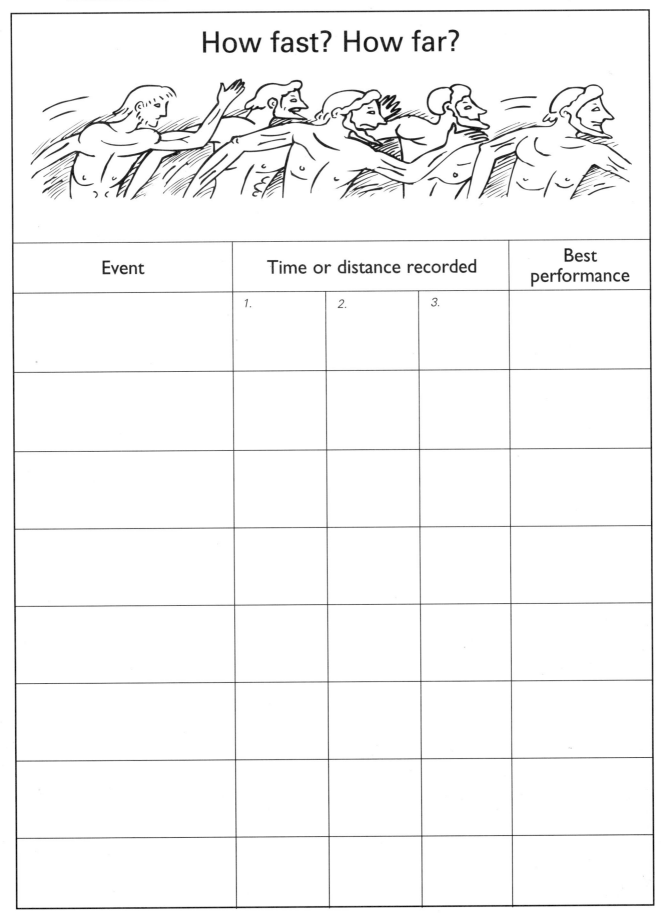

Event	Time or distance recorded			Best performance
	1.	*2.*	*3.*	

Performing a standing jump

Parachute games (1)

Making waves

With each child holding onto the edge with two hands, encourage them all to gently lift and lower the chute, making it billow like waves. (This takes practice to synchronise.) Encourage a whole-body action as the arms are lifted and lowered to and from waist height.

Parachute pass

With everyone holding on to the edge of the chute with two hands, ask them to pass it gently clockwise and then anticlockwise, all keeping in time.

Umbrella

Ask everyone to hold on to the edge of the chute with two hands, at floor level. Ask the children to reach up to full height and then let go of the chute, watching the ripples and billowing shapes as it slowly descends. Encourage the children to sink slowly as the chute does.

Mushroom

Start with everyone in a crouched position, holding on to the edge of the chute with two hands. Ask the children to rise up slowly onto tiptoes, lifting the edge of the chute until it is held above their heads, with everyone in a full-body stretch. While the canopy is inflated, ask the children to step inside the dome created.

Parachute games (2)

Parachute

Everyone holds the edge of the chute with both hands and makes waves. When one person shouts *Parachute*, they all lift their arms above their heads so that the chute inflates and billows above them.

Meet your partner

While the chute is inflated, two children at a time walk to the centre of the chute to shake hands with their partner before returning to their place to hold on to the edge.

    All the children could let go of the chute at the same time and freeze in place as they let it fall on them. They could crawl slowly to the edge.

Letting go together

Everyone pulls on the edge of the chute with two hands (so it is taut), while it is on the floor. On the *Go* signal, they let go and watch it spring towards the centre.

Parachute games (3)

Big wheel

Everyone holds on to the edge of the chute with two hands and walks round, holding the parachute at waist level. Encourage them to get gradually faster, until the chute is whirling round, and then gradually slow down.

Repeat this, walking in the other direction or holding on with one hand, gradually slowing down.

Skydivers

Give children around the chute a number from 1 to 5. They all raise and lower the chute. When their group number is called, those children go under the chute and lie down face up (holding hands), in the form of a star – like skydivers. The remaining children shake the chute up and down on them for a minute or so, their number is called again and they return to their places and another group number is called.

Matching pairs (1)

thunder

lightning

table

chair

pencil

paper

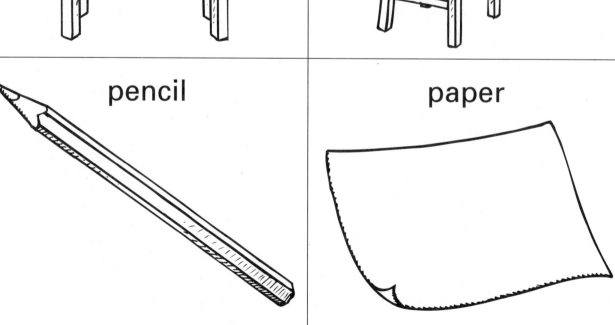

OUTDOOR AND ADVENTUROUS ACTIVITIES: Points of the compass
Can we find features on a map? Page 106
PHOTOCOPIABLE

Matching pairs (2)

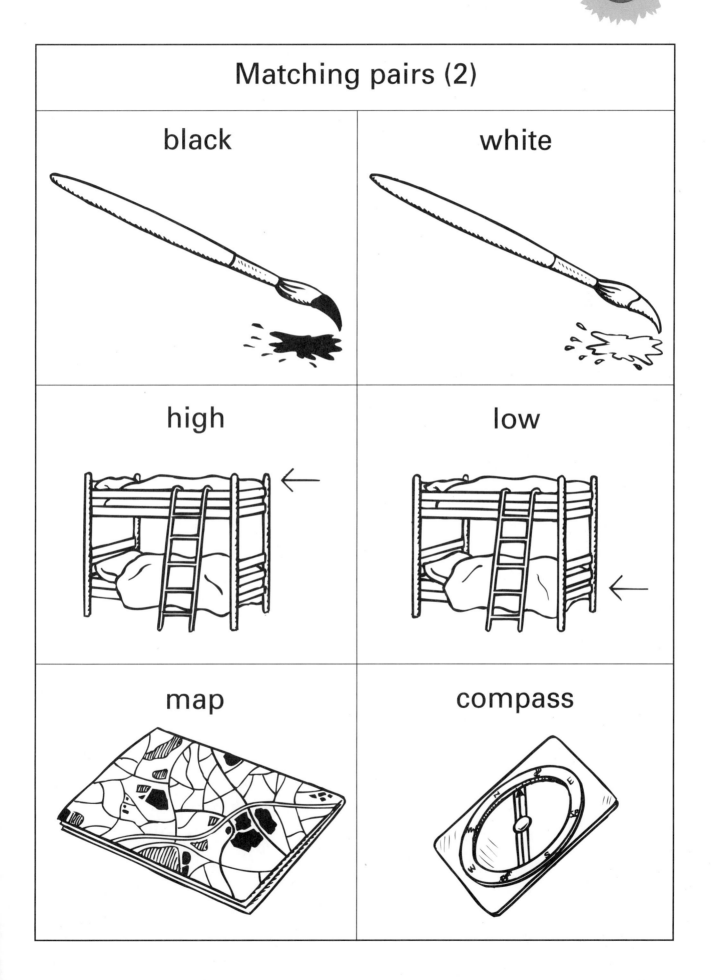

black

white

high

low

map

compass

PHOTOCOPIABLE

OUTDOOR AND ADVENTUROUS ACTIVITIES: Points of the compass
Can we find features on a map? Page 106

Matching pairs (3)

cup

saucer

socks

shoes

knife

fork

Activity trails (1)

How many objects?
Hide objects (such as beanbags or stickers) around the playground. Using a map of the playground, the children, in pairs, endeavour to find as many of the objects as possible. Ensure that they do not remove the objects, but simply mark the place where they are hidden on their map.

Treasure hunt
Choose something to be treasure, such as apples, or something that a group of children can share between them. Hide the treasure in the playing area, and devise simple clues to help the children search for it. As they follow their clues, encourage them to mark on their map the path they have taken, and ultimately, where they found the treasure.

Scavenger hunt
With a map of the playing area between two, ask the children to mark on it some of the features that are not currently identified, such as trees, waste bins, seats and so on.

Leaf hunt
This is the essentially the same as the scavenger hunt, but this time, the children's task is to mark six different varieties of tree on their map.

Activity trails (2)

Action trail

Ask groups of five or six children to collect six cones, skittles or beanbags to use as markers, and set up a trail. Each group must plan and then set up their trail with 10, 20, 30 or 40 metres between each marker in any order. Using a metre rule as a guide, they should pace out the distances between each marker. Two of the runs must be north and south, and the children need to clearly mark the start and the finish.

One runner leads the way around the trail, choosing a different action for each section (fast run, jog, hop, giant strides, side-step and so on).

Encourage the children to take it in turns to lead, with the rest of the team watching and following once the leader has reached the first marker. Time the actions of each team member and the group as a whole.

If they are finding this too easy, add an exercise at each marker (ten star jumps, ten tuck jumps and so on).

Measurement trail

With a map of the playground, including some features highlighted and numbered, ask pairs of children to measure those items (height of waste bin, width of bench and so on), and to record their results.

Information trail

With a map of the area, some features highlighted and numbered, ask the children in pairs to write down certain information (*What is the telephone number? Who is the cook? What does the poster advertise?* and so on).

OUTDOOR AND ADVENTUROUS ACTIVITIES: **Points of the compass**

Can we direct a partner to the treasure? Page 111 and Can we use compass points to find the treasure? Page 113　**PHOTOCOPIABLE**

Compass run instructions

You will need: five beanbags, a metre rule and a stopwatch.

Setting up

1 Choose a space and place one beanbag as the centre spot.
2 Measure ten metres to each of the compass points, and place a beanbag down as a marker at each of the four points.

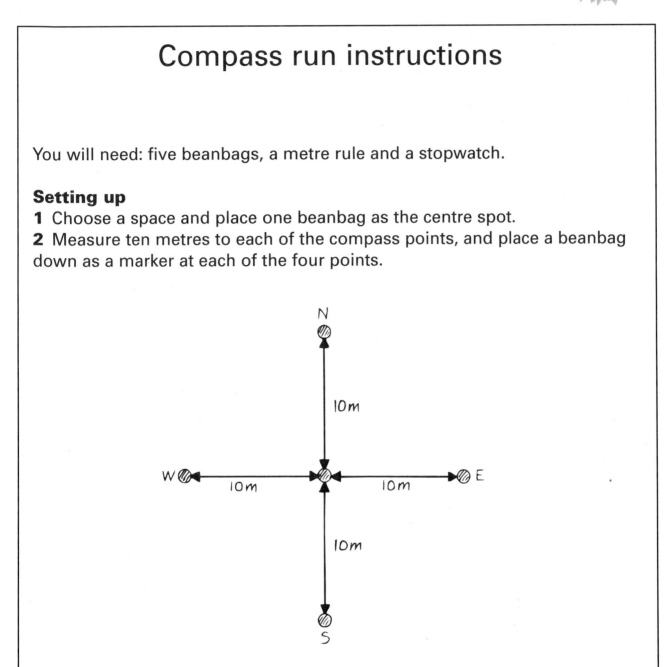

Task

● In groups of four or five, take it in turns to run the compass run. Time one runner at a time.
● Starting at the centre, the runner runs to touch each point of the compass, returning to the centre each time.
● Mark on the results sheet the individuals' times and the time for the group as a whole.

This activity has been modified from the Ten Step Award.

OUTDOOR AND ADVENTUROUS ACTIVITIES: **Points of the compass**

Can we direct a partner to the treasure? Page 111 and Can we use compass points to find the treasure? Page 113

Group _____

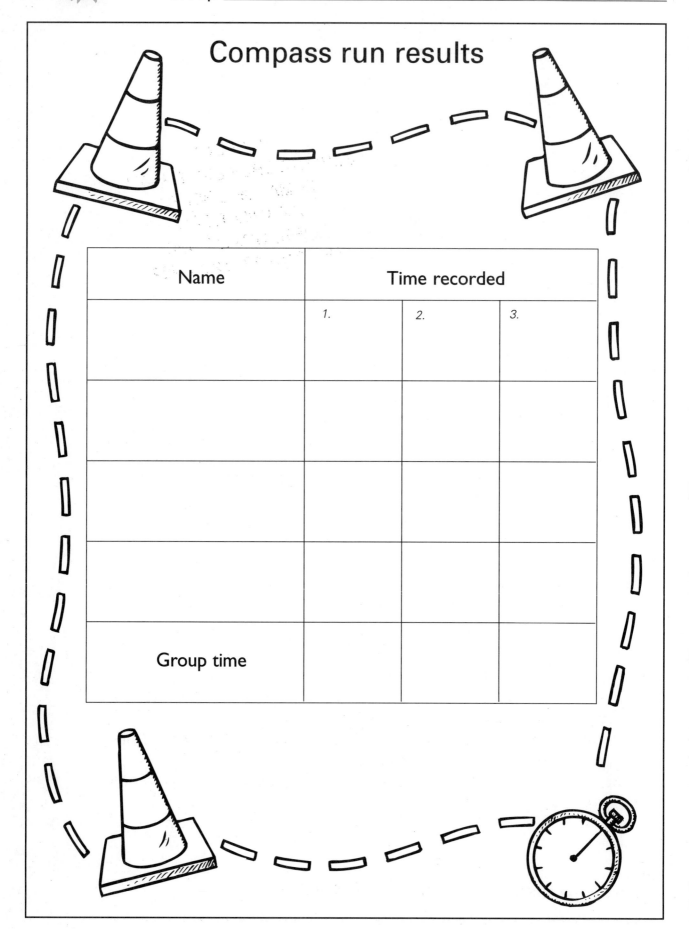

Compass run results

Name	Time recorded		
	1.	2.	3.
Group time			